Hiking Mojave National Preserve

Help Us Keep This Guide Up to Date

Every effort has been made by the authors and editors to make this guide as accurate and use-ful as possible. However, many things can change after a guide is published—trails are rerouted, regulations change, techniques evolve, facilities come under new management, etc.

We would love to hear from you concerning your experiences with this guide and how you feel it could be improved and kept up to date. While we may not be able to respond to all com-ments and suggestions, we'll take them to heart, and we'll also make certain to share them with the authors. Please send your comments and suggestions to the following address:

> The Globe Pequot Press
> Reader Response/Editorial Department
> P.O. Box 480
> Guilford, CT 06437

Or you may e-mail us at:

> editorial@GlobePequot.com

Thanks for your input, and happy trails!

Hiking Mojave National Preserve

15 Day and Overnight Hikes

Bill and Polly Cunningham

FALCONGUIDES ®

GUILFORD, CONNECTICUT
HELENA, MONTANA
AN IMPRINT OF THE GLOBE PEQUOT PRESS

FALCONGUIDES®

Falcon and FalconGuides are registered trademarks of Morris Book Publishing, LLC.

Text design by Nancy Freeborn
Maps created by XNR Productions Inc. © Morris Book Publishing, LLC
All interior photos by Polly and Bill Cunningham

Library of Congress Cataloging-in-Publication Data
Cunningham, Bill, 1943–
  Hiking Mojave National Preserve/Bill and Polly
  Cunningham. — 1st ed.
    p. cm.
  Includes index.
  ISBN 978-0-7627-4465-7
  1. Hiking—California—Mojave National Preserve—
  Guidebooks. 2. Mojave National Preserve (Calif.)—
  Guidebooks. I. Cunningham, Polly. II. Title.
  GV199.42.C22M655 2006
  796.5109794—dc22

                                        2006026151

Manufactured in the United States of America
First Edition/First Printing

To buy books in quantity for corporate use
or incentives, call **(800) 962–0973**
or e-mail **premiums@GlobePequot.com**.

To the thousands of citizens from California and elsewhere, past and present, who laid the groundwork for protection of a large portion of the California desert and to the dedicated state and federal park rangers and naturalists charged with stewardship of California's irreplaceable desert wilderness.

Contents

Acknowledgments

This book could not have been written without the generous assistance from knowledgeable park staff. Special thanks to Kirsten Talken, district interpreter at Mojave National Preserve; and Ramon Sanchez and Thom Thompson, interpretive rangers at Providence Mountains State Park and Mitchell Caverns National Preserve. Even after all this time, we fondly remember the wonderful hot shower Ramon provided for us during our visit to Providence, our first in several days of desert exploration.

During our most recent field trips we had the pleasure of working with James Woolsey, chief of interpretation and outreach for Mojave National Preserve. Not only did he provide many helpful suggestions and ideas, but he also guided us to several magical places in Mojave that appear in this book, including Lava Tubes and Castle Peaks. It was truly wonderful to hike into the Mojave wilderness with James as companion, friend, and guide. In addition, MNP ranger Christina Burns provided an incredibly detailed review of our manuscript, offering numerous suggestions for improvements.

Our thanks also to all the hospitable folks who provided advice and insights during our treks in the desert. Please know that you are not forgotten.

Thanks to you all!

Introduction

The California desert covers the southeastern quarter of our most populous and most ecologically diverse state. Incredibly, three of the four desert subregions that make up most of the arid southwest corner of North America are found within the California desert. These subregions—the Colorado (called the Sonoran in Mexico), Mojave, and Great Basin Deserts—differ by climate and distinct plant and animal communities.

The geographer's definition of a desert as a place with less than 10 inches average annual rainfall says little about what a desert really is. Deserts are regions of irregular and minimal rainfall, so much so that for most of the time, scarcity of water is limiting to life. Averages mean nothing in a desert region that may go one or two years without *any* rain only to receive up to three times the annual average the following year.

In the desert, evaporation far exceeds precipitation. Temperatures swing widely between night and day. This is because low humidity and intense sun heat up the ground during the day, but almost all the heat dissipates at night. Daily temperature changes of 50 degrees or more are common—which can be hazardous to unprepared hikers caught out after dark.

Sparse rainfall means sparse vegetation, which in turn means naked geological features. Most of the California desert is crisscrossed with mountain ranges, imparting an exposed, rough-hewn, scenic character to the landscape. Rather than having been uplifted, the mountains were largely formed by an east-west collision of the earth's tectonic plates, producing a north-south orientation of the ranges. Some would call the result stark, but all would agree that these signatures on the land are dramatic and, at times, overpowering. This very starkness tends to exaggerate the drama of space, color, relief, and sheer ruggedness.

Despite sparse plant cover, the number of individual plant species in the California desert is amazing. At least 1,000 species are spread among 103 vascular plant families. Equally amazing is the diversity of bird life and other wildlife on this deceptively barren land. Many of these birds and animals are active only at night, or are most likely seen during the hotter months at or near watering holes. Hundreds of bird species and more than sixty kinds of reptiles and amphibians fly, nest, crawl, and slither in habitat niches to which they have adapted. Desert bighorn sheep and the rare mountain lion are at the top of the charismatic mega-fauna list, but at least sixty other species of mammals make the desert their home—from kit foxes on the valley floors to squirrels on the highest mountain crests. The best way to observe these desert denizens is on foot, far from the madding crowd, in the peace and solitude of desert wilderness.

The Mojave Desert is the smallest of the four North American deserts and lies mostly in southeastern California. Elevations range from below sea level to around

4,000 feet, with average elevations of 3,000 feet in the rugged eastern portion, which includes the Mojave National Preserve. The hottest temperature ever recorded in the United States—134 degrees—was in the Mojave Desert at Death Valley. Summer temperatures usually exceed 100 degrees, but winter can bring bitter cold, with temperatures sometimes dropping near zero in valleys where dense, frigid air settles at night. Plant cover is typified by Joshua trees, creosote bushes, white bursage, and indigo bushes.

Mojave and other desert parks receive many international visitors who are drawn to the desert because there is no desert in their homeland. Many come during the peak of summer to experience the desert at its hottest. Regardless of whether the visitor is from Europe, a nearby California town, or someplace across the nation, the endlessly varied desert offers something for everyone. Unlike snowbound northern regions, the California desert is a year-round hiker's paradise. There is no better place in which to actually see the raw, exposed forces of land-shaping geology at work. Those interested in history and paleoarchaeology will have a field day. And the list goes on. This book is designed to enhance the enjoyment of all who wish to sample the richness of Mojave National Preserve on their own terms. Travel is best done on foot, with distance and destination being far less important than the experience of getting there.

The Meaning and Value of Wilderness

Visitors to the Mojave Preserve and other desert wildlands should appreciate the meaning and values of wilderness, if for no other reason than to better enjoy their visits with less impact on the wildland values that attracted them in the first place. Nearly 14 percent of California (almost fourteen million acres) is designated federal wilderness, making the Golden State the premier wilderness state in the continental United States. The California Desert Protection Act of 1994 doubled the wilderness acreage in the state and tripled the amount of wilderness under National Park Service jurisdiction, increasing from two million to six million acres.

Those who know and love wild country have their own personal definition of wilderness, heartfelt and often unexpressed, which varies with each person. But since Congress reserved to itself the exclusive power to designate wilderness in the monumental Wilderness Act of 1964, it is important that we also understand the *legal* meaning of "wilderness."

The most fundamental purpose of the Wilderness Act is to provide an *enduring* resource of wilderness for this and future generations so that a growing, increasingly mechanized human population does not occupy and modify every last wild niche. Just as important as preserving the land is the preservation of natural processes, such as naturally ignited fire, erosion, landslides, and other forces that shape the land. Before 1964 the uncertain whim of administrative fiat was all that protected wilderness. During the 1930s the "commanding general" of the wilderness battle, Wilderness Society cofounder Bob Marshall, described wilderness as a "snowbank melting on a hot June day." In the desert the analogy might be closer to a sand dune shrinking on a windy day.

The act defines wilderness as undeveloped federal lands "where the earth and its community of life are untrammeled by man, where man is a visitor who does not remain." In old English the word "trammel" means a net, so "untrammeled" conveys the idea of land that is unnetted or uncontrolled by humans. Congress recognized that no land is completely free of human influence, going on to say that wilderness must "generally appear to have been affected primarily by the forces of nature, with the imprint of man's work substantially unnoticeable." Further, a "wilderness" must have outstanding opportunities for solitude or primitive and unconfined recreation, and be at least 5,000 acres in size or large enough to preserve and use in an unimpaired condition. Also, wilderness may contain ecological, geological, or other features of scientific, educational, scenic, or historical value. The Mojave National Preserve meets and easily exceeds these legal requirements. Any lingering doubts are removed by the distant music of a coyote beneath a star-studded desert sky, or by the soothing rhythm of an oasis waterfall in a remote canyon.

In general, wilderness designation protects the land from development such as roads, buildings, motorized vehicles, and equipment, and from commercial uses except preexisting livestock grazing, outfitting, and the development of mining claims and leases validated before the 1984 cutoff date in the federal Wilderness Act. The act set up the National Wilderness System and empowered three federal agencies to administer wilderness: the Forest Service, the Fish and Wildlife Service, and the National Park Service. The Bureau of Land Management was added to the list with passage of the 1976 Federal Land Policy and Management Act. These agencies can and do make wilderness recommendations, as any citizen can, but only Congress can set aside wilderness on federal lands. This is where politics enters in, epitomizing the kind of grassroots democracy that eventually brought about passage of the landmark California Desert Protection Act. The formula for wilderness conservationists has been and continues to be "endless pressure endlessly applied."

But once designated, the unending job of wilderness stewardship is just beginning. The managing agencies have a special responsibility to administer wilderness in "such manner as will leave them (wilderness areas) unimpaired for future use and enjoyment *as wilderness.*" Unimpairment of wilderness over time can only be achieved through partnership between concerned citizens and the agencies.

Wilderness is the only truly biocentric use of land. It is off-limits to intensive human uses with an objective of preserving the diversity of nonhuman life, which is richly endowed in the California desert. As such, its preservation is our society's highest act of humility. This is where we deliberately slow down our impulse to drill the last barrel of oil, mine the last vein of ore, or build a parking lot on top of the last wild peak. The desert wilderness explorer can take genuine pride in reaching a remote summit under his or her power, traversing a narrow serpentine canyon, or walking across the uncluttered expanse of a vast desert basin. Hiking boots and self-reliance replace motorized equipment and push-button convenience, allowing us to find something in ourselves we feared lost.

Have Fun and Be Safe

Wandering in the desert has a reputation of being a dangerous activity, thanks to both the Bible and Hollywood. Usually depicted as a wasteland, the desert evokes fear. With proper planning, however, desert hiking is not hazardous. In fact, it is fun and exciting and is quite safe.

An enjoyable desert outing requires preparation. Beginning with this book, along with the maps suggested in the hike write-ups, you need to be equipped with adequate knowledge about your hiking area. Carry good maps and a compass, and know how to use them.

Calculating the time required for a hike in the desert defies any formula. Terrain is often rough; extensive detours around boulders, dry falls, and drop-offs mean longer trips. Straight-line distance is an illusion. Sun, heat, and wind likewise all conspire to slow down even the speediest hiker. Therefore, distances are not what they appear in the desert. Five desert miles may take longer than 10 woodland miles. Plan your excursion conservatively, and always carry emergency items in your pack (see appendix B).

While you consult the equipment list (appendix B), note that water ranks the highest. Carrying the water is not enough—take the time to stop and drink it. This is another reason desert hikes take longer. Frequent water breaks are mandatory. It's best to return from your hike with empty water bottles. You can cut down on loss of bodily moisture by hiking with your mouth closed and breathing through your nose; reduce thirst also by avoiding sweets and alcohol.

Driving to and from the trailhead is statistically far more dangerous than hiking in the desert backcountry. But being far from the nearest 911 service requires knowledge about possible hazards and proper precautions to avoid them. It is not an oxymoron to have fun and to be safe. Quite to the contrary: If you're not safe, you won't have fun. At the risk of creating excessive paranoia, here are the treacherous twelve:

Dehydration

It cannot be overemphasized that plenty of water is necessary for desert hiking. Carry one gallon per person per day in unbreakable plastic screw-top containers. And pause often to drink it. Carry water in your car as well so you'll have water to return to. As a general rule, plain water is a better thirst-quencher than any of the colored fluids on the market, which usually generate greater thirst. It is very important to maintain proper electrolyte balance by eating small quantities of nutritional foods throughout the day, even if you feel you don't have an appetite.

Changeable Weather

The desert is well known for sudden changes in the weather. The temperature can change 50 degrees in less than an hour. Prepare yourself with extra food and clothing, rain/wind gear, and a flashlight. When leaving on a trip, let someone know your exact route, especially if traveling solo, and your estimated time of return; don't forget to let them know when you get back. Register your route at the closest park office or back-country board, especially for longer hikes that involve cross-country travel.

Hypothermia/Hyperthermia

Abrupt chilling is as much a danger in the desert as heat stroke. Storms and/or night-fall can cause desert temperatures to plunge. Wear layers of clothes, adding or sub-tracting depending on conditions, to avoid overheating or chilling. At the other extreme, you need to protect yourself from sun and wind with proper clothing. The broad-brimmed hat is mandatory equipment for the desert traveler. Even in the cool days of winter, a delightful time in the desert, the sun's rays are intense.

Vegetation

You quickly will learn not to come in contact with certain desert vegetation. Cat-claw, Spanish bayonet, and cacti are just a few of the botanical hazards that will get your attention if you become complacent. Carry tweezers to extract cactus spines. Wear long pants if traveling off-trail or in a brushy area. Many folks carry a hair comb to assist with removal of cholla balls.

Rattlesnakes, Scorpions, Tarantulas

These desert "creepy crawlies" are easily terrified by unexpected human visitors, and they react predictably to being frightened. Do not sit or put your hands in dark places you can't see, especially during the warmer "snake season" months. Carry and know how to use your snakebite-venom-extractor kit for emergencies when help is far away. In the event of a snakebite, seek medical assistance as quickly as possible. Keep tents zipped and always shake out boots, packs, and clothes before putting them on.

Mountain Lions

The California desert is mountain-lion country. Avoid hiking at night when lions are often hunting. Instruct your children on appropriate behavior when confronted with a lion. Do not run. Keep children in sight while hiking; stay close to them in areas where lions might hide.

Mine Hazards

The California desert contains thousands of deserted mines. All of them should be considered hazardous. Stay away from all mines and mine structures. The vast majority of these mines have not been secured or even posted. Keep an eye on young or adventuresome members of your group.

Hanta Virus

In addition to the mines, there are often deserted buildings around the mine sites. Hanta virus is a deadly disease carried by deer mice in the Southwest. Any enclosed area increases the chances of breathing the airborne particles that carry this life-threatening virus. As a precaution, do not enter deserted buildings.

Flash Floods

Desert washes and canyons can become traps for unwary visitors when rainstorms hit the desert. Keep a watchful eye on the sky. Never camp in flash-flood areas. Check at a ranger station on regional weather conditions before embarking on your back-country expedition. A storm anywhere upstream in a drainage can result in a sudden torrent in a lower canyon. Do not cross a flooded wash. Both the depth and the current can be deceiving; wait for the flood to recede, which usually does not take long.

Lightning

Be aware of lightning, especially during summer storms. Stay off ridges and peaks. Shallow overhangs and gullies should also be avoided because electrical current often moves at ground level near a lightning strike.

Unstable Rocky Slopes

Desert canyons and mountainsides often consist of crumbly or fragmented rock. Mountain sheep are better adapted to this terrain than us bipeds. Use caution when climbing; the downward journey is usually the more hazardous. Smooth rock faces such as in slickrock canyons are equally dangerous, especially when you've got sand on the soles of your boots. On those rare occasions when they are wet, the rocks are slicker than ice.

Giardia

Any surface water, with the possible exception of springs where they flow out of the ground, is apt to contain *Giardia lamblia,* a microorganism that causes severe diarrhea. Boil water for at least five minutes or use a filter system. Iodine drops are not effective in killing this pesky parasite.

Zero-Impact Desert Etiquette

The desert environment is fragile; damage lasts for decades—even centuries. Desert courtesy requires us to leave no evidence that we were ever there. This ethic means no grafitti or defoliation at one end of the spectrum, and no unnecessary footprints on delicate vegetation on the other. Here are seven general guidelines for desert wilderness behavior:

Avoid making new trails. If hiking cross-country, stay on one set of footprints when traveling in a group. Try to make your route invisible. Desert vegetation grows very slowly. Its destruction leads to wind and water erosion and irreparable harm to the desert. Darker crusty soil that crumbles easily indicates cryptogamic soils, which are a living blend of tightly bonded mosses, lichens, and bacteria. This dark crust prevents wind and water erosion and protects seeds that fall into the soil. Walking can destroy this fragile layer. Take special care to avoid stepping on cryptogamic soil.

Keep noise down. Desert wilderness means quiet and solitude, for the animal life as well as other human visitors.

Leave your pets at home. Check with park authorities before including your dog in the group. Better yet, share other experiences with your best friend, not the desert.

Pack it in/pack it out. This is more true in the desert than anywhere. Desert winds spread debris, and desert air preserves it. Always carry a trash bag, both for your trash and for any that you encounter. If you must smoke, pick up your butts and bag them. Bag and carry out toilet paper (it doesn't deteriorate in the desert) and feminine hygiene products.

Never camp near water. Most desert animals are nocturnal, and most, like the bighorn sheep, are exceptionally shy. The presence of humans is very disturbing, so camping near their water source means they will go without water. Camp in already-used sites if possible to reduce further damage. If none is available, camp on ground that is already bare. And use a camp stove. Ground fires are forbidden in most desert parks; gathering wood is also not permitted. Leave your campsite as you found it. Better yet, improve it by picking up litter, cleaning out fire rings, or scattering ashes of any inconsiderate predecessors. Remember that artifacts fifty years old or older are protected by federal law and must not be moved or removed.

Treat human waste properly. Bury human waste 4 inches deep and at least 200 feet from water and trails. Pack out toilet paper and feminine hygiene products; they do not decompose in the arid desert. Do not burn toilet paper; many wildfires have been started this way.

Respect wildlife. Living in the desert is hard enough without being harassed by human intruders. Remember this is the only home these animals have. They treasure their privacy. Be respectful and use binoculars for long-distance viewing. *Especially important:* Do not molest the rare desert water sources by playing or bathing in them.

Beyond these guidelines, refer to the regulations provided in the preserve overview for specific rules governing backcountry usage. Enjoy the beauty and solitude of the desert, and leave it for others to enjoy.

How to Use This Book

This guide is *the* source book for those who wish to experience on foot the very best hikes and backcountry trips the Mojave National Preserve has to offer. Hikers are given many choices from which they can pick and choose, depending on their wishes and abilities.

The maps in this book that depict a detailed close-up of an area use elevation tints, called hypsometry, to portray relief. Each gray tone represents a range of equal elevation, as shown in the scale key with the map. These maps will give you a good idea of elevation gain and loss. The darker tones are lower elevations and the lighter grays are higher elevations. The lighter the tone, the higher the elevation. Narrow bands of different gray tones spaced closely together indicate steep terrain, whereas wider bands indicate areas of more gradual slope.

Maps that show larger geographic areas use shaded, or shadow, relief. Shadow relief does not represent elevation; it demonstrates slope or relative steepness. This gives an almost 3-D perspective of the physiography of a region and will help you see where ranges and valleys are.

For a general geographic orientation, begin with the overview map in the next section. Here you'll find the locations of the hikes. The numbering of the hikes generally runs south to north, although this is sometimes altered by the clustering of hikes sharing common access.

Refer to the "Hikes at a Glance" matrix for a quick overview of all of the hikes presented for the preserve. After making your selections, turn to the specific hike descriptions for added detail. Each hike is numbered and named and begins with a general description. This overview briefly describes the type of hike and highlights the destination and key features.

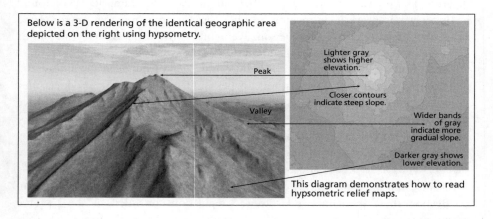

Below is a 3-D rendering of the identical geographic area depicted on the right using hypsometry.

Peak

Lighter gray shows higher elevation.

Closer contours indicate steep slope.

Valley

Wider bands of gray indicate more gradual slope.

Darker gray shows lower elevation.

This diagram demonstrates how to read hypsometric relief maps.

The "start" is the approximate road distance from a nearby town or park visitor center to the trailhead. The idea is to give you a mental picture of where the hike is in relation to your prospective travels.

Hike "distance" is given in total miles for the described route. The mileage is in one direction for a loop, in which you return to the place where you started without retracing your steps, or for a one-way hike, in which you begin at one trailhead and end at another, requiring two vehicles, a shuttle bus, or another driver to pick you up or deposit you at either end. Round-trip mileage is provided for an out-and-back hike, in which you return to the trailhead the same way you came. A lollipop loop combines a stretch of out-and-back with a loop at one end. Mileages were calculated in the field and double-checked as accurately as possible with the most detailed topographic maps.

"Approximate hiking time" provides a best guess as to how long it will take the average hiker to complete the route. Always add more time for further exploration or for contemplation.

The "difficulty" rating is necessarily subjective, but it is based on the authors' extensive backcountry experience with folks of all ages and abilities. Easy hikes present no difficulty to hikers of all abilities. Moderate hikes are challenging to inexperienced hikers and might tax even experienced hikers. Strenuous hikes are extremely difficult and challenging, even for the most-seasoned hikers. Distance, elevation gain and loss, trail condition, and terrain were considered in assigning the difficulty rating. There are, of course, many variables. The easiest hike can be sheer torture if you run out of water in extreme heat—a definite no–no.

"Trail surfaces" are evaluated based on well-defined trail standards. Dirt trails have no obstructions and are easy to follow. Rocky trails may be partially blocked by slides, rocks, or debris but are generally obvious and easy to find. Primitive trails are faint, rough, and rocky and may have disappeared completely in places. In the desert some of the best hiking takes place on old four-wheel-drive mining roads that are now closed to vehicular use because of wilderness designation or to protect key values, such as wildlife watering holes. Many of the desert hikes are off-trail in washes, canyons, ridges, and fans. "Use trails" may form a segment of the route. A use trail is simply an informal, unconstructed path created solely by the passage of hikers.

The best "season" is based largely on the moderate-temperature months for the particular hike and is greatly influenced by elevation. Additional consideration is given to seasonal road access at higher altitudes. The range of months given is not necessarily the best time for wildflowers, which is highly localized and dependent on elevation and rainfall. Nor is it necessarily the best time to view wildlife, which may be during the driest and hottest summer months near water sources.

The maps listed are the best available for route-finding and land navigation: the relevant 7.5-minute topographic map (1:24,000 scale or 2.6 inches = 1 mile) with a 40-foot contour interval. These U.S. Geological Survey maps can be purchased for $6.00 each (price as of this writing) directly from Map Distribution, USGS Map Sales, Box 25286, Federal Center, Building 810, Denver, CO 80225; by calling (800) ASK–USGS; or online at www.usgs.gov/pubprod/. See appendix C for a listing of other useful smaller-scale maps.

For more information on the hike, the best available "trail contact" for the park management agency is listed. See appendix D for a complete listing of all agency addresses and phone numbers.

"Finding the trailhead" includes detailed up-to-date driving instructions to the trailhead or jumping-off point for each hike. For most hikes, there is no formal trailhead but rather a starting point where you can park. To follow these instructions, start with the beginning reference point, which might be the park visitor center, a nearby town, or an important road junction. Pay close attention to mileage and landmark instructions. American Automobile Association (AAA) map mileages are used when available, but in many instances we had to rely on our car odometer, which may vary slightly from other car odometers.

The text following the driving directions is a narrative of the actual route with general directions and key features noted. In some cases interpretation of the natural and cultural history of the hike and its surroundings is included. The idea is to provide accurate route-finding instructions, with enough supporting information to enhance your enjoyment of the hike without diminishing your sense of discovery— a fine line indeed. Some of these descriptions are augmented with photographs that preview a representative segment of the hike.

The trail itinerary, "Miles and Directions," provides detailed mile-by-mile instructions while noting landmarks, trail junctions, canyon entrances, dry falls, peaks, and historic sites along the way.

And last, please don't allow our value-laden list of "favorite hikes" (appendix A) to discourage you from completing any of the other hikes. They're all worth doing!

Map Legend

Boundaries

	National wilderness/preserve boundary
	National park boundary
	State park boundary
	County park boundary
—·—·—	State boundary

Transportation

⑮	Interstate
⑨⑤	U.S. highway
⑥②	State highway
S22	Primary road
	Other road
	Unpaved road
= = = = =	Unimproved road
	Featured unimproved road
	Featured trail
··············	Optional trail
- - - - - - -	Other trail
+++++++	Railroad
•—•—•—	Power line

Hydrology

	Intermittent stream
	Spring
	Fall
	Lake
	Dry lake
	Lava bed
	Sand/wash

Physiography

×	Spot elevation
)(	Pass
▲	Peak
∩	Cave
⊔⊔⊔	Cliff

Symbols

🚶	Trailhead
START	Trail start
❷	Trail locator
↻	Trail turnaround
P	Parking
🚻	Restroom/toilet
⌂	Campground
▲	Backcountry campground
♦	Lodging
?	Visitor center
👥	Ranger station
☎	Telephone
🚏	Picnic area
○	Town
👁	Overlook
■	Point of interest
⚒	Mine/prospect
•—•	Gate
⋈	Bridge
+▬	Airport/landing strip

Mojave National Preserve

B ig and empty" aptly describes Mojave National Preserve, which, at 1.6 million acres, makes up 10 percent of the entire Mojave Desert region in its eastern end. The dry landscape we see now is the product of a wetter past, with ancient sedimentary rocks from what was once an ocean floor preserved by the stark aridity of today's climate. The preserve is a varied mix of jagged peaks, colorful serpentine canyons, booming sand dunes, volcanic cinder cones, dry lake beds, historic mines, rock art by Paleo-Indians, and vast expanses framed by the largest concentration of Joshua trees in the world.

In 1976 Congress established the California Desert Conservation Area, directing the Bureau of Land Management (BLM) to come up with a management plan for the half of this twenty-five-million-acre region that is in the public domain. As a result, BLM set up the 1.5-million-acre East Mojave National Scenic Area in 1980. Unfortunately, the East Mojave continued to be impacted by indiscriminate off-road vehicle use, mining, overgrazing, and wanton vandalism. Greater protection was called for, but the wheels of politics sometimes turn slowly. In 1986 U.S. senator Alan Cranston of California first introduced the California Desert Protection Act, but passage took the same amount of time required for the 1964 Wilderness Act—eight long years! The act transferred the East Mojave from the BLM to the National Park Service and upgraded the designation from administrative "scenic area" to statutory "preserve."

"Preserve" rather than park status for Mojave means the continuation of preexisting hunting in accordance with state regulations. Mojave National Preserve is the only National Park Service unit in the California desert where hunting is permitted. As an added safety precaution, hikers should wear hunter's orange or other bright colors when hiking in the preserve during the fall hunting season. Other "grandfathered" uses include mining preexisting claims and cattle grazing. The OX Cattle Company (a major grazing permittee) is a colorful remnant of the Old West, with origins traceable to 1888. The historic OX Ranch headquarters in the Lanfair Valley has been sold to the National Park Service. Indeed, livestock grazing seems marginal at best in this sparsely vegetated land. Of the more than a dozen original grazing allotments in the preserve, all but one have been retired.

Geologic Signatures on the Landscape

When visiting the preserve, one can look in any direction and be reminded of Mojave's geologic past—a land molded by earthquakes, fault lines, sinking valleys, and rising mountains formed by the tearing apart of the earth's crust. Domes, cinder cones, and lava beds tell the tale of volcanic eruptions of monumental proportions. The Mojave Desert was uplifted around 140 million years ago by pressure from plates of the earth's crust grinding against one another. Seventy million years of erosion reduced an astounding 20,000 to 25,000 feet of sedimentary rock to gently sloping terrain. The mountain ranges of Mojave were uplifted along rows of faults about thirty million years ago as continental plates collided. During a wetter time, about eighteen million years ago, Mojave resembled African savannahs with large herds of grazing animals.

As recently as 15,000 years ago, the Mojave River flowed aboveground into the now-gone Lake Manly in Death Valley. After the last ice age, roughly 10,000 years ago, the climate became much drier. This is partly because the Mojave Desert sits in the rain shadow of the lofty Sierra Nevada and other ranges to the south and west. Cinder cone activity dates back 7.6 million years to 8,000 years ago, but lava flows took place as recently as 800 to 1,000 years ago just west of Cima Dome—a huge 1,500-foot-high symmetrical mound of ancient granite exposed by erosion.

Life in the Desert

Elevations in the preserve range from around 800 feet to the nearly 8,000-foot summit of Clark Mountain, supporting a corresponding diversity of plants and animals. The most common shrub at lower elevations, the creosote bush is a perfectly adapted desert survivor with narrow, resinous leaves that prevent water loss. As the older stems in the plant's center die, a cloned ring of new stems is formed that can live for hundreds of years. Creosote bushes are able to completely tap surrounding soil moisture, which effectively keeps away competing vegetation. Above 3,000 feet the dark gray bark of the intricately branched blackbrush gives the land a dark, somber look. Joshua trees are prevalent here on well-drained gravel plains. These members of the yucca family are usually the largest plants in their landscape. Their branches seem to lift upward like the arms of the biblical prophet Joshua—hence the name given by early Mormon settlers. Spanish bayonet and the larger Mojave yucca are also common in this mid-elevational range. Piñon-juniper woodlands occur at still higher elevations, in such exposed places as the rocky slopes of the rugged New York and Providence Mountains.

◀ *A climber pauses for a look at the view from Table Mountain.*

The old OX Ranch was recently acquired by the National Park Service.

Mojave National Preserve is home to a seldom-seen but rich array of fauna—mammals, birds, insects, and reptiles, all of which are adapted to lack of water and intense heat. Coyotes are abundant, although you will not see and hear as many in the ranching country of East Mojave as you would in Death Valley or Joshua Tree. The abundance of rodents and rabbits can be determined as easily by looking up as down: Raptors are commonly seen riding the air currents, seeking their prey. Several small bands of desert bighorn sheep keep a sharp eye out for the predatory mountain lion in secluded mountains and canyons. One of the more distinguished denizens is the threatened desert tortoise. Protection of tortoise habitat was one of the most compelling arguments for passage of the California Desert Protection Act, so much so that someone placed a tortoise on President Clinton's desk when he signed the bill into law on October 31, 1994.

Human History

Paleo-Indians likely lived and hunted in the Mojave region around the end of the last ice age, 10,000 to 14,000 years ago. As the climate became drier, these people made greater use of seeds, nuts, and roots for food. The more recent native peoples of the Mojave included the Chemehuevi, who were the southernmost band of Piutes. The harshness of the land kept this population of hunter-gatherers small. The petroglyphs we see today throughout Mojave are largely the product of more ancient peoples who predated the Chemehuevi. A good example of this artistry is found near Piute Creek along the Mojave Trail. Archaeologists believe that some of the rock art comprises tribal clan markings of territory or trails.

The Mojave Trail was a route for both early Native American trading and European travel into the region. In 1776 a Spanish priest named Francisco Garces became the first European to visit what is now the Mojave National Preserve. Following the Mojave Trail, Garces and his tribal guides traveled past Piute Creek, the New York and Providence Mountains, and Kelso Dunes. The first American to traverse the Mojave was the renowned trapper Jeddediah Smith. Smith made the difficult journey in 1826 and then again a year later in a much shorter time by traveling at night to escape the scorching 120-degree summer heat. The route was again followed in 1857 by Edward Beale, who laid out a wagon road along the Mojave Trail. Beale achieved notoriety by using camels as pack stock. After the road was completed, the camels were turned loose in the desert and eventually died off. During the 1860s primitive army outposts were built along the road about a day's travel apart. These outposts, such as the one at Piute Creek, were abandoned in 1868 when the overland mail route was rerouted away from the Mojave Road.

Miners swarmed into the region in the 1870s, leaving countless prospect adits, tunnels, and shafts, but the mines didn't boom until the railroad arrived in 1883. Ten years later a 30-mile short-line railroad from Goffs north to the New York Mountains replaced the Mojave Road as a freight route. The railroad served both mining and a developing cattle industry, which somehow survives to this day. Homesteaders came into the East Mojave around 1910 during a series of wet years, but most had left by 1925 after the normal dry weather resumed.

Park Regulations and Facilities

The Mojave National Preserve is one of the newest, largest, least developed, and least regulated of all of the units in the National Park System. Sensitive and respectful visitor use will go a long way toward keeping regulations to a minimum, which is a goal of the National Park Service in the preserve. Mojave National Preserve is one of the few units in the National Park System without an entrance fee. However, the National Park Service is likely to institute a fee in 2008. Check with a Mojave National Preserve office or the Web site (www.nps.gov/moja) for details.

Nearly half of the preserve, some 700,000 acres, is designated wilderness in twenty-two separate units. Some of the boundaries near roads and washes have been posted. Please respect the wilderness by doing everything possible to lessen the impact of your visit. The desert is at once both rugged and fragile. No off-road

vehicular travel is allowed, so please keep vehicles on designated routes. As with the other parks, vehicles must be street legal. Heavy rains during the winter and spring of 2005 adversely impacted most preserve roads. Thus, four-wheel drive is recommended for all unmaintained dirt roads, which provide the only vehicular access for many of the hikes.

At this time the National Park Service is continuing the long tradition of open-desert camping in the preserve. Car camping is allowed at backcountry sites with existing fire rings next to secondary roads. If you're camping beyond the road, backcountry permits are not required. The only requirements are to camp at least 0.25 mile from any water source to avoid disturbing wildlife, and to set up camp off the trail a minimum of 0.5 mile from any road or developed area. Please follow zero-impact practices and carry out all trash.

There are only seven developed trails in the preserve. A 2-mile (one-way) trail to Teutonia Peak on Cima Dome takes off from a signed trailhead on the Cima Road south of Interstate 15. An 8-mile (one-way) trail between Hole-in-the-Wall and Mid Hills Campgrounds can be reached from either campground. The Lake Tuendae Nature Trail is a 0.25-mile round-trip from the Zzyzx parking area on the west end of the preserve. The Rings Trail is a short but challenging 30-minute out-and-back descent into Banshee Canyon using metal rings bolted into the rock. A short nature trail with signs identifying desert plants connects the Hole-in-the-Wall Campground to the Hole-in-the-Wall Information Center. Quail Basin and Kelso Dunes are also developed trails.

There are two developed fee campgrounds in the preserve and one in the state recreation area. The Hole-in-the-Wall (HITW) Campground (thirty-five sites) and adjacent Information Center are 18 miles north of Interstate 40 on Black Canyon Road. The Mid Hills Campground (twenty-six sites) is 25 miles north of I–40, 2 miles off Black Canyon Road. The Providence Mountains Campground (six sites) is 17 miles northwest of I–40 at the end of Essex Road. All three are open year-round on a first-come, first-served basis. Fire pits are provided, but if you want a fire, bring wood with you; collecting or cutting wood in the desert is not allowed. Water, vault-toilets, trash containers, and picnic tables are available year-round at the two park campgrounds. The HITW Campground also has a dump station. The Black Canyon Equestrian and Group Campground is located across the road from the HITW Information Center and Campground. Reservations are accepted for group camps only and are required; call HITW at (760) 928–2572. The HITW Information Center offers seasonal visitor programs and has public telephones. Educational materials are available at HITW and the Kelso Depot Information Center. There are no services in the preserve—no stores, gas, or motels—so bring everything you need. As always when traveling in the desert, bring plenty of water.

◀ *North of mile 1 on the Hole-in-the-Wall to Mid Hills hike.*

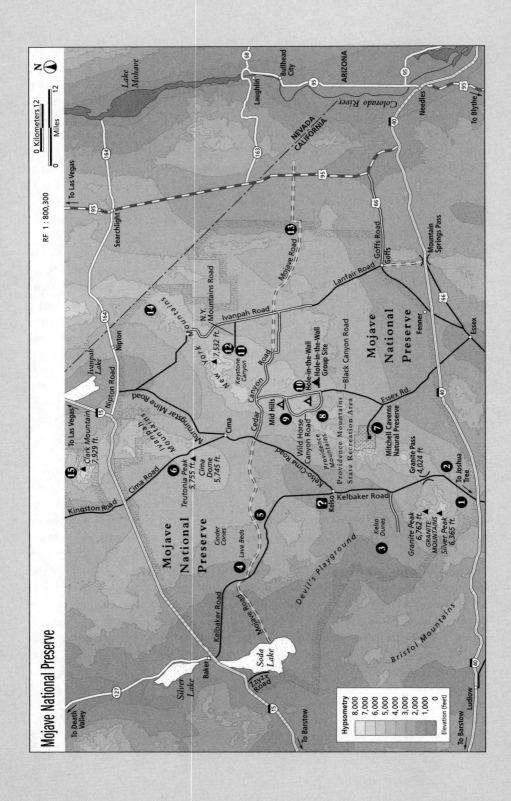

Mojave National Preserve

RF 1 : 800,300

0 Kilometers 12

0 Miles 12

N

The park service has recently refurbished the historic Kelso Depot in the heart of the preserve to its original 1924 condition. It is now a beautiful visitor information and education center and a major attraction in its own right. This facility, known as the Kelso Depot Information Center, opened officially in December 2005 and is an excellent starting point for exploring Mojave National Preserve.

It may be tempting to feed wildlife but remember that "a fed animal is a dead animal." Wild creatures must remain wild if they are to survive. All elements of the environment—plants, cultural and historical artifacts, rocks—are protected so that they can be enjoyed by others. Pets must be confined or kept on a short leash but may join you anywhere in the preserve. Better yet, leave them at home so that both they and you can have a better time. Although legal hunting is allowed in season, target shooting is not.

The exterior boundaries of the preserve contain a large amount of private inholdings. It is important to obey NO TRESPASSING signs, close gates, and, in general, respect private property.

Providence Mountains State Recreation Area

In 1956 the State of California acquired the Mitchell Caverns from the Mitchell family. Subsequent land transfers from the BLM have increased the park to its present 5,900 acres along the rugged eastern slopes of the Providence Mountains, encompassed within the south-central portion of the preserve. To safeguard wildlife, only day use is allowed outside the campground. The Mitchell Caverns are the only limestone caves in the California park system and can only be visited with a guided ranger tour. The 1.5-mile hike/tour takes one-and-a-half to two hours and is offered one to three times a day depending on season and day of the week. There is one short nature trail near the visitor center/campground, plus a longer trail to Crystal Spring that leads to the edge of the backcountry, high in the Providence Mountains (see Hike 7).

How and When to Get There

The "lonesome triangle" of the Mojave National Preserve is bounded on the north by Interstate 15 and on the south by I–40. These two interstate highways join in Barstow, about 50 miles west of the preserve. The paved Kelbaker Road crosses the preserve from Baker south to I–40, halfway between Barstow and Needles. The paved Kelso-Cima Road takes off from Kelso Depot and heads north to I–15. The National Park Service has restored the historic Kelso Depot to mint condition. This grand old building and its grounds are a must-see attraction between hikes. Several shorter paved roads and improved dirt roads access major mountain ranges and points of interest. The closest major commercial airport is 50 miles northeast of the preserve at Las Vegas. There are no motels or service stations in the preserve and very few close by. Don't drive into the preserve without plenty of gas, food, area maps, and water. Services are available in surrounding communities, such as Needles on the east, Barstow on the west, and Baker to the north on I–15. Cell phone service is unreliable.

Rifle deer season is mid–October to early November, with quail season continuing until the end of January.

From the standpoint of hiking comfort, October through May is generally the best season to visit the preserve. Summer daytime temperatures typically exceed one hundred degrees. Depending on winter and early-spring rains, wildflowers burst forth in a splash of color from March through May.

We continue to recommend USGS maps as the best and most detailed maps available for the Mojave area, however, they are not sold at the Mojave National Preserve Visitor Centers. Order USGS maps by calling (888) ASK–USGS or online at www.usgs.gov/pubprod/.

Mojave National Preserve Hikes at a Glance

Hike (Number)	Distance	Difficulty*	Features	Page
Caruthers Canyon (11)	3.0 miles	M	canyon, mine site	54
Castle Peaks (14)	6.6 miles	M	spires, vista	65
Clark Mountain/				
North Canyon (15)	4.4 miles	M	mountain canyon	68
Clark Mountain summit	10.0 miles	S	vista, peak	71
Crystal Spring Overlook (7)	2.2 miles	M	spring, vista	40
Eagle Rocks (9)	2.0 miles	E/M	boulders, vista	48
Fort Piute/Piute Gorge (13)	7.0 miles	M/S	historic site, archaeology, gorge	61
Hole-in-the-Wall to Mid Hills (8)	8.4 miles	M/S	vistas	43
Kelso Dunes (3)	3.0 miles	M/S	dunes, vista	28
Keystone Canyon (12)	3.8 miles	M	canyon, flora	57
Lava Tube (5)	1.5 miles	E	cave, cinder cones	34
North Lava Bed Wash (4)	2 miles	E	geology, archaeology	31
Quail Spring Basin (2)	5.9 miles	M	boulders, vistas	26
Silver Peak (1)	9.6 miles	S	vista, peak	23
Table Top Mountain Loop (10)	7.0 miles	S	vista, peak	50
Teutonia Peak/Cima Dome (6)	4.0 miles	M	vista	37

*E=easy, M=moderate, S=strenuous

1 Silver Peak

Silver Peak provides a spectacular view of south-central Mojave. The vista from the 6,365-foot mountaintop in the Granite Mountains is a panorama of the desert landscape. In addition to being part of Mojave National Preserve, the Granite Mountains also have special recognition as a nature preserve. Tread lightly.

Start: About 45 miles southeast of Baker.
Distance: 9.6 miles out and back.
Approximate hiking time: 6 to 8 hours.
Difficulty: Strenuous.
Trail surface: Dirt two-track; use trail to summit.

Seasons: October through June.
USGS topo map: Bighorn Basin-CA (1:24,000).
Trail contact: Kelso Depot Information Center (see appendix D).

Finding the trailhead: From Interstate 40, 77.5 miles east of Barstow and 64 miles west of Needles, take the Kelbaker Road exit north into the preserve. At 10.1 miles north of the freeway exit, take the unmarked dirt road on the left (west) of Kelbaker. There is another dirt road almost opposite this one going east on the other side of Kelbaker. Four-wheel drive is recommended for this dirt road that leads west 1.8 miles to a small plateau, where a wilderness boundary post marks the end of motorized use. Park there. This spot is also an excellent car campsite.

The Hike

From the parking area, you can see the highest point on the western horizon, Silver Peak, your destination. The view from that point is magnificent, but the journey to get there is no less spectacular. Please keep in mind that some of the land here is owned by the Granite Mountains Research Center, which is conducting long-term research. Do not disturb any study plots or remove flagging in the area. The trail is deteriorating and provides challenging but enjoyable hiking. Turnout promontories provide respite from the steep ascent, plus panoramic views. There may be evidence of wild burros in the valley.

The trail ends at 4.6 miles, at an elevation of 6,075 feet. Even if you do not go on to the summit, there's a great view from here. To reach the summit of Silver Peak, follow the trail as it winds around the mountain and climbs 300 feet in its final 0.2-mile climb—it is quite strenuous. Your efforts are rewarded when you reach the rocky summit, especially if it is a clear day.

The change in altitude on this hike results in a wide variety of desert plants, from the creosote-sage scrub at the parking area and throughout the lower valley to increasing cholla and eventually to piñon-juniper woodlands. Any hiker will also certainly notice the desert's ability to erase the evidence of past uses; the trail upon which you travel is a prime example. The remnants of cattle ranching are scattered around and are deteriorating rapidly. This is a wilderness area that has earned that label.

The journey back the way you came is excellent for its scenery, too, looking out

A hiker enjoys the view eastward from the slopes of Silver Peak.

at the southern extension of the Providence Mountain range. In the valley below you will see the entire trail as it goes nearly straight east to the parking area. Once you reach the alluvial fan and then the canyon floor, the trail surface becomes very gentle. We completed this leg of the hike in the dark (with the help of a half-moon), and, except for the catclaw, it was easy going.

Miles and Directions

0.0 Take any of the three dirt two-tracks (all banned to vehicles) off the plateau; they converge in the wash below. Head west toward the Granite Mountains up Cottonwood Wash.

0.2 Pass through 12-foot gate posts and come to a fork. Take the fainter (right) trail.

3.0 The trail enters the canyon, framed by huge boulders. Plow through the Mormon tea as you continue to follow the trail.

3.2 Continue to hike straight up the slight shelf, looking at the trail 50 yards ahead/above.

4.6 At trail's end, the use trail to Silver Peak is marked by cairns.

4.8 Follow the trail as it winds around the mountain in its final 0.2-mile climb to the summit.

9.6 Make your descent, then retrace your route back to the trailhead.

Silver Peak; Quail Spring Basin

RF 1 : 63,600

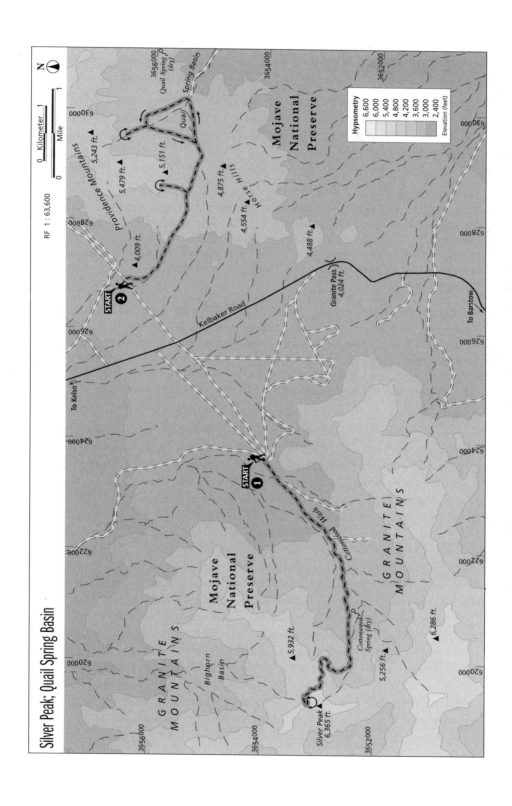

2 Quail Spring Basin

This basin hike is an easy lollipop loop with two side trips around granite formations with opportunities for climbing boulders and peaks. Immense monzogranite boulder mounds dot the route. You'll enjoy the views of the Granite Mountains and the Kelso Dunes.

See map on page 25.
Start: About 45 miles southeast of Baker.
Distance: 5.9-mile lollipop (side trips of 0.5 mile and 0.6 mile; additional distance for investigating the granite mounds).
Approximate hiking time: 3 to 4 hours.
Difficulty: Moderate.

Trail surface: Dirt path.
Seasons: October through May.
USGS topo map: Van Winkle Spring-CA (1:24,000).
Trail contact: Kelso Depot Information Center (see appendix D).

Finding the trailhead: From Interstate 40, 77.5 miles east of Barstow and 64 miles west of Needles, take the Kelbaker Road exit north into the preserve. About 10 miles from the freeway exit, there is a dirt road on your right (east). There is another dirt road almost immediately across Kelbaker heading west at this spot. Four-wheel drive is recommended for this dirt road, which winds to the east 0.9 mile to the wilderness boundary post on the right. This marks the end of vehicular use. The parking area has been improved and the trailhead is signed.

The Hike

This hike in the south end of the Providence Mountains takes you on a gentle slope up from the valley floor, enabling you to see the panorama of this central Mojave region without climbing a mountain. The view of the Kelso Dunes, the Granite Range, and the Providence Mountains makes the first 2 miles of the hike (and the last 2) most spectacular. Closer at hand, the first section of the hike travels through brittlebush and creosote bushes, with mounds of monzogranite piled in fantastic shapes as a backdrop to the east. These are soaring boulders in a cathedral–like setting, and vertical columnar granite reaches hundreds of feet over you. In addition to their size, the boulders have been eroded into imaginative shapes, producing holes and caverns as well as cartoon representations of mice, skulls, and faces.

The peaks of these granite mountains look impressive as you hike up the rise from the parking area, but the loftiest one is in the back row and can be viewed (and climbed, if you wish) from the eastern valley. Plenty of other bouldering activity exists for those who are not enticed by the peak. These large dollops of granite ice cream have a superb gritty yet firm surface for scrambling.

From the trailhead, the trail rises gently on the alluvial fan. A fork at 1.5 miles provides an opportunity to explore granite boulders by turning left on a short dead end. Return to the main trail and continue over the high point on the ridge (4,350 feet) and drop to the fork at mile 2, where the return loop comes back on the left. Continue east into Quail Spring Basin. At mile 2.5 a basalt outcropping on your left marks the wash/trail where you turn and begin to climb northwest toward the notch in the Providence Range. As you continue to the junction at mile 3.4, the lofty granite spires become more awesome. At the junction, a side trip to the right takes you up a rocky gorge. For the very ambitious hiker, this would be the route to the loftiest peak (5,479 feet) above the basin. Your return to the trailhead follows the trail to the left back to the major intersection at mile 2. Magnificent vistas and fascinating rock formations are numerous throughout your trek with or without side trips.

Miles and Directions

0.0 Climb the gentle alluvial fan from the trailhead.

1.5 At the fork explore to the left, then follow the right-hand trail.

1.9 Cross the low pass over the ridge.

2.0 At the fork the left trail is the return loop. Take the right trail.

2.5 At the basalt outcropping, go left up the wash/trail.

3.4 At the high point of the loop hike, turn right for access to the peak, left to meet the main trail.

3.9 Intersect the main trail and turn right.

5.9 Complete the loop hike back at the trailhead.

3 Kelso Dunes

This trailless romp through a sand dunes ecosystem to a dune summit is a unique experience for your visit to Mojave. The golden sand dunes contrast dramatically with the surrounding rocky mountains and desert.

Start: About 40 miles southeast of Baker.
Distance: 3 miles out and back.
Approximate hiking time: 2 hours.
Difficulty: Moderate; strenuous to the top of the dunes.

Trail surface: Sand. No trail. Line-of-sight cross-country sand dune route.
Seasons: October through April.
USGS topo map: Kelso-CA (1:24,000).
Trail contact: Kelso Depot Information Center (see appendix D).

Finding the trailhead: From Interstate 40, 77.5 miles east of Barstow and 64 miles west of Needles, take Kelbaker Road north 15.3 miles to signed Kelso Dunes Road on your left. Drive west 3 miles on the improved dirt road to the second parking area where there is a vault toilet and exhibits on desert ecology and wildlife. The trail to the dunes is directly behind these.

The Hike

The Kelso Dunes were created by 10,000 to 20,000 years of unrelenting winds, sending the sand of the Mojave River delta into these ever-changing formations. This landform (created by wind) is actively moving, but only back and forth due to the contrary wind pattern. At times these dunes "sing" or "boom," something that only 10 percent of the world's dunes can do.

The mountain ranges nearby represent violent volcanic activity. The dunes contrast sharply with the surrounding topography by their softly rounded shapes and their rosy glow. The fine sand consists of rose quartz, feldspar, and magnetite. The quartz gives it the rosy color. The magnetite produces a black-stripe effect on the windswept ridges of the dunes.

Not an arid wasteland, the dunes are home to more than one hundred species of plants and many animals. The tracks of the latter—kangaroo rats, sidewinders, kit foxes, and scorpions, among others—are visible along your hike. The dunes are also home to the Kelso Jerusalem cricket, which exists nowhere else.

Follow the hiker-established foot trail as best as possible as you go northwest to the most westerly dune. The hike to the base of this hill is moderate, rising only 250 feet in 1 mile. For an ascent of the dune—a strenuous 0.5-mile climb—hike to the saddle east of the tall dune, and then hike westerly up the ridge to its apex (3,000 feet). From this lofty spot, you can enjoy spectacular views of the Devil's Playground

A hiker reaches the 3,000-foot summit ▶
of Kelso Dunes.

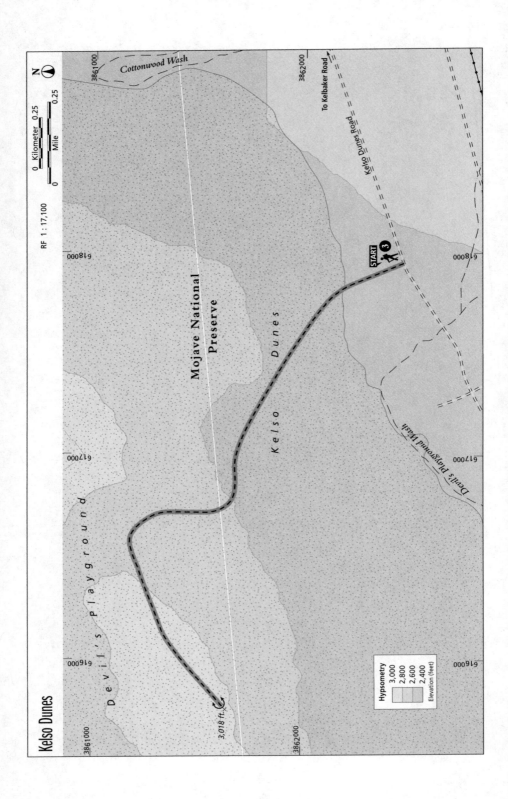

Kelso Dunes

RF 1 : 17,100

N

0   Kilometer   0.25

0   0.25
                     Mile

Cottonwood Wash

Devil's Playground

3,018 ft.

Mojave National Preserve

Kelso Dunes

Devil's Playground Wash

START
3

Kelso Dunes Road

To Kelbaker Road

Hypsometry
3,000
2,800
2,600
2,400
Elevation (feet)

to the north and the Providence Range to the east. The dimensions of the Kelso Dunes are impressive and are best seen in all their vastness from this high spot.

Hiking back, try to retrace your steps in order to minimize damage to the fragile dune environment.

4 North Lava Bed Wash

This outing in the lava beds gets you up close to these interesting igneous rock formations. In addition to geology, this hike provides a glimpse of both the history and prehistory of the region in that the profile of the lava beds abuts a narrow turn of the historic Mojave Road.

Start: About 14 miles southeast of Baker.
Distance: About a 2-mile lollipop or out and back.
Approximate hiking time: 1 to 2 hours.
Difficulty: Easy.
Trail surface: Rocky dirt path, clear wash, lava rock, primitive burro trail; cross-country segment for the loop.

Seasons: October through April.
USGS topo map: Indian Spring-CA (1:24,000).
Trail contact: Kelso Depot Information Center (see appendix D).

Finding the trailhead: From Baker on Interstate 15, drive south on Kelbaker Road for 14.1 miles to the first major wash on the left (east), which is the trailhead. This point is also 22.4 miles northwest of Kelso on Kelbaker Road and 0.4 mile north of the only gap in these lava hills. The trailhead is unsigned, but there is a large place to park just off the east side of the highway, adjacent to a prominent outcropping of lava rock.

The Hike

Start by climbing up toward the large outcrop of lava above and to the right of the trailhead. About 30 feet up and just below the lava wall, you'll pick up a faint trail, partly overgrown, that parallels the cliff face for about 0.5 mile. The slow but usable trail provides a good introduction to volcanic geology along this northern edge of the vast lava–bed region of the northwestern Mojave National Preserve. Especially interesting is the cutaway lava cliff face, which exposes the profile of the rock along with a colorful display of red, green, and gray lichens on the lava formations. The historic Mojave Road makes a sharp turn at this point. The Mojave Road was first used by Native Americans and later developed by the military to encourage settlement in the region.

There is a surprising array of desert plants in this austere lunarscape. You'll see barrel cacti, desert holly, bursage, yucca, creosote, chicory, beavertail, and various

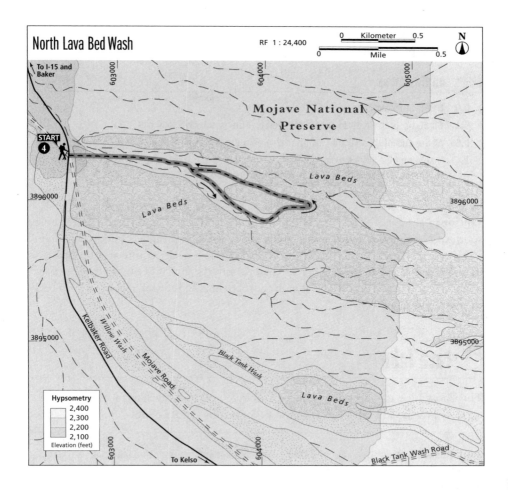

North Lava Bed Wash

RF 1 : 24,400

0 — Kilometer — 0.5
0 — Mile — 0.5

N

To I-15 and Baker

Mojave National Preserve

START 4

Lava Beds

Lava Beds

3896000

3896000

3895000

3895000

Kelbaker Road

Willow Wash

Mojave Road

Black Tank Wash

Lava Beds

Hypsometry
2,400
2,300
2,200
2,100
Elevation (feet)

To Kelso

Black Tank Wash Road

cholla cacti to name only a few. You may also see chuckwalla, rattlesnakes, horned lizards, kangaroo rats, black-throated sparrows, and desert tortoise.

At 0.5 mile the cliff trail ends at a jumbled lava talus slope. To add more variety to this overland route, climb up to the plateau to the immediate right (south), which you can also do at the beginning of the hike. Make a circle cross-country of a mile or more into the interior of the lava flow. You can gradually angle around back into the main wash. Depending on where you rejoin the wash, you may come across a distinctive turnaround point for the hike. The wash opens up into a wide sandy oval encircled by smooth, gray stone and dark, deeply eroded lava. A side wash narrows up and to the right, but the main wash lies above a 20-foot dry gray stone/lava rock waterfall that can be easily climbed. From the dry fall the mostly clear wash can be

◀ *Looking east along a vertical lava cliff wall above the wash.*

easily followed for about 0.6 mile back down to the trailhead to complete this brief lava–beds exploration.

Miles and Directions

0.0 Begin at the trailhead.

0.1 Climb up to the right to a primitive trail just below the lava rock cliff.

0.5 At the end of the cliff trail, climb (right) onto the adjacent plateau/ridge.

1.4 Hike along the ridge cross-country; drop to the left (north) back to the wash, and hike 0.6 mile back down the wash to complete the loop.

2.0 Return to the trailhead.

Option: *Lava Flow*—This hike begins and ends in Black Tank Wash, about 1.5 miles south of North Lava Bed Wash on Kelbaker Road. The unsigned trailhead contains a large parking area just to the east of Kelbaker Road near the intersection of Black Tank Wash and the historic Mojave Road. Climb the lava wall on either side of the wash and wander across the lava flow into its fascinating interior, making a loop back to the trailhead.

5 Lava Tube

This short hike to—and down into—a unique volcanic cavelike formation can be extended to the reddish–black moonscape of nearby cinder cones.

Start: About 25 miles southeast of Baker.
Distance: 1.5 miles out and back.
Approximate hiking time: 1 to 2 hours.
Difficulty: Easy.
Trail surface: Dirt use trail to tubes; rocky cross-country route to cones.

Seasons: November through April.
USGS topo map: Indian Spring-CA (1:24,000).
Trail contact: Kelso Depot Information Center (see appendix D).

Finding the trailhead: From Baker on Interstate 15, drive south on Kelbaker Road for 19.9 miles and turn left (north) onto the unsigned Aikens Mine Road. Continue north for 4.8 miles to the first junction. Turn left and drive about 0.2 mile to a corral with a large area for parking. From Kelso in the south, drive north on Kelbaker Road, 14 miles to Aikens Mine Road. Depending on road conditions, four-wheel drive may be advisable because of areas of deep sand.

The Hike

Follow an old road for about 0.25 mile north and then watch on the right for the narrow trail to the lava tube entrance. A narrow steel ladder allows for a careful descent of some 20 feet to the floor of a main cavern chamber. The ladder is not

Park interpreter James Woolsey descends into a lava tube.

maintained, so enter cautiously at your own risk. The lava tube was formed when an ancient volcano erupted, causing a rapid flow of lava. The outer flow took longer to cool than the inner flow, forming this cavelike opening in the earth. Bring a head-lamp or flashlight and be prepared for an area with a low ceiling that requires stoop walking or hands-and-knees crawling to access the larger cave. You may see bats as well as ropy strands of pahoehoe lava on the cave walls. If you explore the tubes during the hot months, you'll love this dark, cool respite from the scorching sun. Watch for snakes near the entrance.

After climbing out of the lava tube, you may want to stretch your legs to the nearest of thirty-two cinder cones that dot this 25,600-acre portion of the preserve, which has been designated a National Natural Landmark. The cones have been dated back some ten million years and are made up of what may be the densest rock on the planet. An easy 1 mile or so of walking from the tubes will get you up and back from the closest cone to the north. The modest rise in elevation to the top of the cone provides an excellent overview of this amazing, eerie landscape.

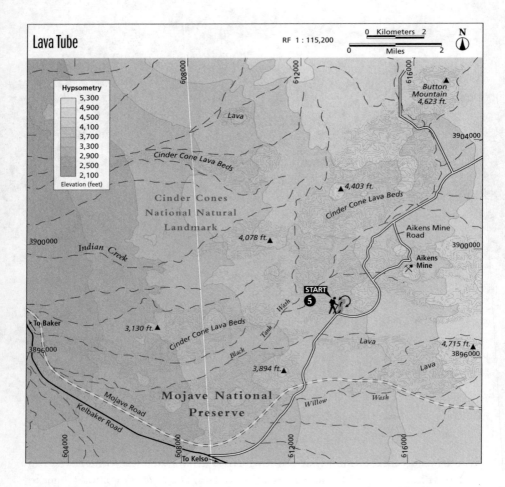

Options: *Aikens Mine*—From the trailhead, return to the main dirt road. Drive north on Aikens Mine Road a few more miles to the closed Aikens Mine, which once excavated lava for home and yard decoration. Although it's an eyesore, the mine does allow you to peer into the inside of a cinder cone.

Willow Wash—This dry willow-lined streambed lies just off Aikens Mine Road. It offers cinder cone vistas and a glimpse into prehistoric times with evidence of early human habitation.

6 Teutonia Peak/Cima Dome

This short but steep out and back on one of only seven maintained trails in the Mojave National Preserve, within the wilderness boundary, ends at a rocky point. From here you look out at an extensive Joshua tree forest. The surrounding volcanic geology is interspersed with mounds of white monzonite. The expansive scenic vistas stretch into the hazy desert infinity.

Start: About 35 miles northeast of Baker.
Distance: 4 miles out and back.
Approximate hiking time: 2 to 3 hours.
Difficulty: Moderate.
Trail surface: Dirt path with rocks on peak section.

Seasons: October through June.
USGS topo map: Cima Dome-CA (1:24,000).
Trail contact: Kelso Depot Information Center (see appendix D).

Finding the trailhead: From Interstate 15, 25 miles northeast of Baker, take the Cima Road exit to the paved Cima Road. Continue southeasterly on Cima Road for 11.2 miles, reaching the signed trailhead parking area with an interpretive sign, on the west side of the road 0.1 mile north of Sunrise Rock. Coming from the south on Kelso-Cima Road, the trailhead is 6.7 miles north of Cima Junction.

The Hike

The Teutonia Peak Trail is one of only seven maintained trails in the entire 1.6-million-acre Mojave National Preserve. The well-signed trailhead contains an informative wildlife/woodland vegetation exhibit. Here you'll learn a bit about the ladder-back woodpecker, Scott's oriole, desert night lizard, night snake, and yucca moth, which pollinates the Joshua tree. The evergreen Joshua tree is not a tree at all but, rather, a striking member of the yucca family. The trail was extensively rehabilitated in 2003 and is now much improved.

For the first 0.5 mile, the sandy, clear trail climbs gently through this vast Joshua tree forest to the first gate, crosses a trail, and continues southwest. At 0.9 mile the trail reaches some old mine tailings and open shafts, the largest of which has been fenced off for public safety. Here the trail changes to a narrower path before coming to a gate and crossing another trail at 1 mile. At 1.1 miles the base of the northwest summit ridge of Teutonia Peak is reached at 5,220 feet. The trail is rocky but in good condition as it ascends a slope of prickly pear, yucca, juniper, and stunted Joshua trees. The final 0.5 mile climbs steeply on a series of rock steps. At 2 miles the trail ends in a notch between two large mounds of monzonite granite, just below the bouldery cliff summit of 5,755-foot Teutonia Peak.

Don't attempt the difficult summit unless you are an experienced rock climber. Instead, spend some time exploring the endless nooks and pockets surrounding the

Teutonia Peak to the southwest.

peak. Teutonia Peak is actually an extensive complex of granite outcroppings, boulders, and huge mounds of monzonite. Walk out on the fairly level ridge to the east to gain an excellent overall perspective of the peak complex and much of the preserve to the north and east. Stunted Joshua trees mix with juniper all the way to this lofty 5,640-foot level.

The end-of-the-trail notch provides a magnificent view southwestward of Cima Dome, which gradually rises 1,500 feet above the surrounding desert to an elevation almost equal to that of Teutonia Peak. The dome is a huge symmetrical hump of monzonite formed when a core of molten rock cooled and hardened deep beneath the surface of the earth. It has since been uncovered by millions of years of erosion, resulting in the unusual landscape we see today. Cima Dome is adorned by the densest Joshua tree forest in the world. These trees are a different, more spindly variety than those found to the south in Joshua Tree National Park.

After you've soaked up the view and enjoyed a bit of exploration around the peak, double-back on the trail to the trailhead to complete this diverse 4-mile round-trip hike/climb.

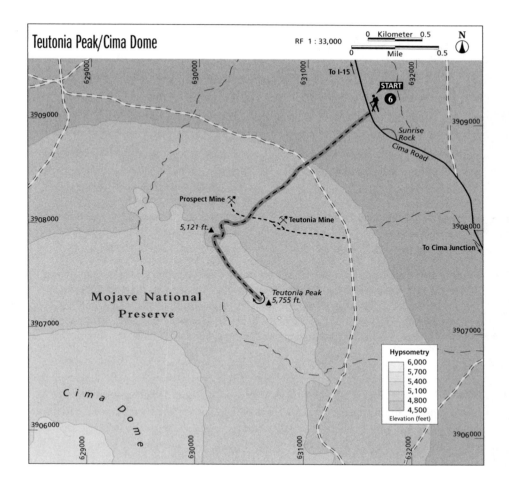

Miles and Directions

0.0 Start at the signed Teutonia Peak trailhead.

0.5 Arrive at the first gate.

0.9 Observe mine shafts and tailings.

1.0 Arrive at the second gate.

1.1 The trail starts up the northwest summit ridge.

2.0 Take in the view from the notch in the rocks, just below the summit.

4.0 Return to the trailhead.

7 Crystal Spring Overlook

This short but steep canyon hike leads to a mountain spring high in the Providence Mountains. Here you'll enjoy towering columns of volcanic rock, sweeping vistas, and a chance to view birds, desert bighorn sheep, and other wildlife.

Start: About 60 miles west of Needles, surrounded by the south-central region of the Mojave National Preserve.
Distance: 2.2 miles out and back.
Approximate hiking time: 1 to 2 hours.
Difficulty: Moderate.
Trail surface: Steep rocky path.

Seasons: October through May (or November through March to avoid rattlesnakes).
USGS topo map: Fountain Peak-CA (1:24,000).
Trail contact: Providence Mountains State Recreation Area and Mitchell Caverns Natural Preserve (see appendix D).

Finding the trailhead: From Interstate 40, take the Essex Road exit, which is 44 miles west of Needles and 100 miles east of Barstow. Drive north on the well-signed, paved Essex Road for 16 miles to the recreation area, visitor center, and campground at the end of the road. The signed trailhead to Crystal Spring is next to the picturesque stone visitor center, which was the residence of Jack and Ida Mitchell from the 1930s through the mid-1950s.

The Hike

The short but steep Crystal Spring trail provides a wonderful introduction to the power and spellbinding beauty of a high desert canyon on the dramatic east slope of the perpendicular Providence peaks. Although steep and rocky in places, the trail is easy to follow to its end, but be careful of catclaw and other spiny vegetation that can snag you along the way. As you climb you'll see the gently graded Mary Beal Nature Trail below and across the canyon.

Within only 0.2 mile the trappings of civilization seem far away with the continuing gain in distance and elevation. The rugged canyon contains an interesting mix of both limestone and volcanic rock, with the reddish volcanic extrusion known as rhyolite being most striking. The rock platform supporting the pipeline Mitchell built to water his resort in the 1930s is still visible across the canyon. The steep rocky hillsides and gullies are densely covered with prickly pear, barrel and cholla cacti, as well as piñon pine and Mojave sagebrush.

With the increase in elevation, there is an increasing sense of entering a relatively lush microenvironment. For the first 0.7 mile, the trail climbs on the left side of the ravine then crosses over to the right side. The trail continues steeply for the next 0.3 mile until coming to the end of the trail at 4,920 feet, just below the spring. To reach

The Crystal Spring trail winds through a ▶
cactus garden at mile 0.3.

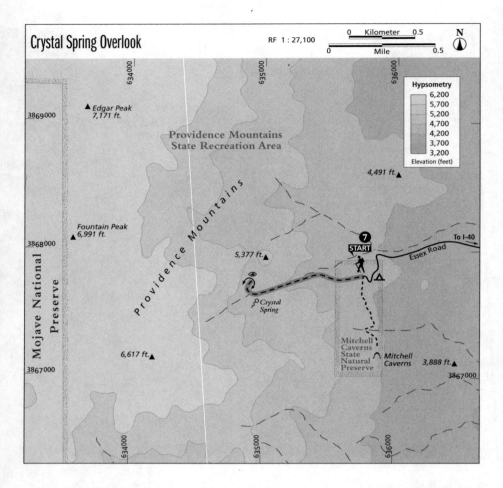

RF 1 : 27,100

the lower end of the spring, continue hiking up a faint use trail on the left side, which climbs and then quickly drops to the grottolike opening of the brush-lined spring. Cross over and climb the opposite slope to an overlook at 1.1 miles.

This 4,960-foot-high viewpoint, next to a jagged column of red rhyolite, is a great place to pause and soak up the view. On a clear day the Hualapai Mountains in Arizona are visible, 105 miles east. More than 300 square miles of the Clipper Valley can be seen, along with the low ridgeline of the ancient Colton Hills basalt, which at 1.8 billion years old is as old as the deepest layer of rock exposed in the Grand Canyon. Take time to feel the power of this secluded canyon but remember that the spring is used by bighorn sheep and other wildlife, so disturbance must be kept to a minimum.

The extremely thick growth of willow and other shrubbery at and above the spring inhibits farther travel directly up the canyon. To complete this 2.2-mile out-and-back hike, retrace your route back to the visitor center.

Miles and Directions

0.0 Begin at the Crystal Spring trailhead (4,300 feet).

0.2 The trail steepens.

0.6 The trail levels out.

0.7 The trail crosses a gully and climbs steeply to the end.

1.0 The trail ends at Crystal Spring (4,920 feet).

1.1 Arrive at the overlook (4,960 feet).

2.2 Return to the trailhead.

Options: From the overlook, it is possible to continue climbing on a strenuous cross-country route to the top of 6,991-foot Fountain Peak or 7,171-foot Edgar Peak along the high crest of the Providence Range. Both summits are six- to ten-hour round-trips and require an early start, good conditioning, and lots of experience in negotiating steep terrain with loose rock. From the overlook, the recommended route heads toward a saddle to the immediate north, then southwest up a prominent ridge for 1.5 miles, and finally angles north another mile to Fountain Peak. Edgar Peak rises another extremely rugged mile to the north.

8 Hole-in-the-Wall to Mid Hills

A hike on one of only seven maintained trails in the preserve leads you across rolling terrain with a deep volcanic canyon and high desert vistas of volcanic plugs, granite mounds, and distant mountains.

Start: About 65 miles northwest of Needles.
Distance: 8.4 miles one way.
Approximate hiking time: 4 to 6 hours.
Difficulty: Strenuous if hiked uphill south to north; moderate if hiked downhill from north to south.

Trail surface: Dirt trail and rocky wash.
Seasons: November through May.
USGS topo map: Columbia Mtn-CA (1:24,000).
Trail contact: Hole-in-the-Wall Information Center (see appendix D).

Finding the trailhead: From Needles, drive 44 miles west on Interstate 40 to the Essex Road exit. Travel 10 miles northwest on Essex Road, then turn right on Black Canyon Road. Drive another 10 miles to Wild Horse Canyon Road. Turn left and continue another mile to the trailhead parking area on the right. For a more secure parking location, you may wish to park at the visitor center and start the hike at the Rings Trail. You may also begin or end the hike at the northernmost point, off Wildhorse Canyon Road across from the Mid Hills Campground.

Looking up into the mouth of Banshee Canyon.

The Hike

Although more difficult, a south-to-north route on this trail, mostly uphill, is recommended for several reasons. First, if you leave during the morning—which you should certainly do given the length of the hike—you'll have the sun at your back rather than in your face, a definite plus during the warmer months. Second, by climbing up into the higher desert, you can better appreciate subtle changes in vegetation and geology in this varied land. But perhaps the best reason is that you will better enjoy the fantastic volcanic geology of Banshee Canyon by dropping into it when fresh early in the day, rather than the other way around. That said, most visitors still prefer to hike downhill from Mid Hills to Hole-in-the-Wall. If you elect to go with the flow, gravity that is, simply reverse the following hike description.

When you get to the "Rings" trailhead at the picnic area, be sure to walk left a short distance to the overlook, protected by a guardrail high above a narrow, pocketed canyon. One of many "holes" can be seen high in a volcanic wall to the south. Some fifteen million years ago, volcanic eruptions spilled layer upon layer of lava and ash here. The mesas seen in this area are isolated remnants of these lava flows. The many holes in the rock are the product of uneven cooling, made larger by erosion. It's a wonderland of caverns, ledges, and openings. The reddish color on the dark gray volcanic rock is caused by oxidation. Wind and moisture continue to mold this unusual landscape.

From the trailhead, the descent into spectacular Banshee Canyon is steep and potentially hazardous. Two sets of steel ring handholds are attached to pins in the rock. Although the rings add an element of safety, great care must be exercised when making the descent. The volcanic walls of the canyon are deeply pocked by erosion. Within 0.2 mile the 215-foot drop to the canyon floor has been achieved. Be on the lookout for snakes in the narrow "Rings" area.

Numerous temptations for side climbing and exploration present themselves. When you're ready, continue down another 0.1 mile to the canyon mouth from where Barber Butte rises impressively to the north. Follow the signed trail across a wash. At 0.5 mile the trail intersects the wash. Bear right and follow a cholla- and yucca-lined wash surrounded by distant mesas. Look back to the sheer cliff walls of the canyon you've just descended.

At 1 mile the trail reaches a signed junction. The Wild Horse Canyon trailhead is 0.25 mile south, and the trail to Mid Hills heads north. Turn right at this junction toward the Mid Hills Campground and continue up a ridge toward a gap in the mesas. Here the trail makes a gradual ascent of an alluvial fan. A wall of dark volcanic rock parallels the trail to the right.

At 1.7 miles a low pass is reached. Dropping down another 0.1 mile, the trail crosses a gate signed 6.2 MILES TO MID HILLS. The mileages on the signs are wrong as often as not. A deep lava canyon wash winds to the left. The steep, rocky trail drops to the wash, where a trail sign points up the wash to the right. A trail junction appears at 2.2 miles; stay right. Striking white cliffs of volcanic ash topped with a dark volcanic crown rise majestically to the left. Another trail junction is met at 2.4 miles; again follow the sign and veer to the right. At 2.5 miles the signed trail leaves the wash and turns left (north), leaving the sweeping mesas to the south. For the next mile, the trail follows a wash and then climbs up a sandy ridge in high, open desert where white, granite boulders begin to dot the landscape.

About one-third of the way up the trail, evidence appears of the Hackberry fire caused by lightning in June 2005. More than 70,000 acres were affected. Although lightning fires are a natural part of ecosystems, it will take many years for the piñon-juniper woodland to recover fully.

At 4.3 miles the trail crosses a dirt road that leads to the tailings of the abandoned Gold Valley Mine, where a working windmill provides water for cattle. For a side trip to the mine/windmill site, turn right at this junction and follow the road southeasterly for 0.5 mile.

Continuing north toward Mid Hills, the trail soon passes through a gate signed 3.8 MILES TO MID HILLS, intersecting another trail. For the next 0.5 mile, the trail climbs

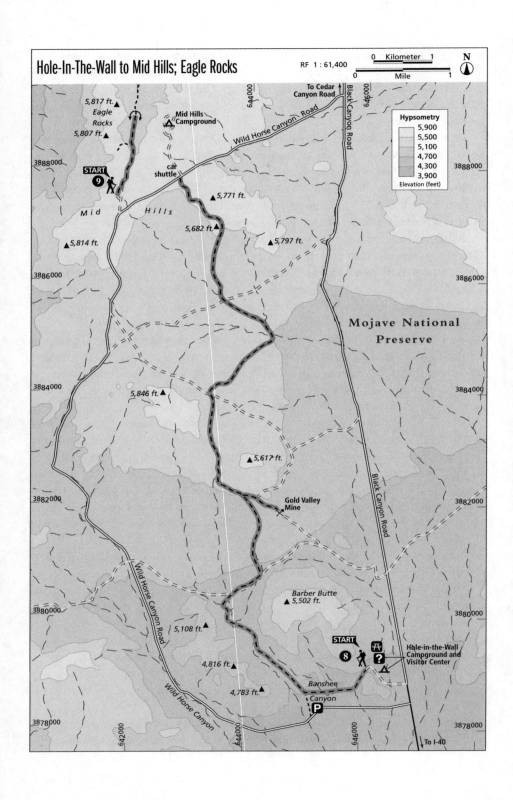

Hole-In-The-Wall to Mid Hills; Eagle Rocks

RF 1 : 61,400

Kilometer

Mile

N

Hypsometry

- 5,900
- 5,500
- 5,100
- 4,700
- 4,300
- 3,900

Elevation (feet)

To Cedar Canyon Road

Wild Horse Canyon Road

Black Canyon Road

5,817 ft. Eagle Rocks

5,807 ft.

Mid Hills Campground

START 9

car shuttle

M i d   H i l l s

5,771 ft.

5,682 ft.

5,797 ft.

5,814 ft.

Mojave National Preserve

5,846 ft.

5,617 ft.

Gold Valley Mine

Wild Horse Canyon Road

Barber Butte
5,502 ft.

5,108 ft.

START 8

Hole-in-the-Wall Campground and Visitor Center

4,816 ft.

4,783 ft.

Banshee Canyon

Wild Horse Canyon

Black Canyon Road

P

To I-40

a small pass from where, at 5,350 feet, a vast juniper-sage plateau opens up ahead with small, pointed peaks and mesas adorning the landscape. At 5 miles the trail crosses another fence, signed MID HILLS 3.1 MILES. Take the signed trail to the right.

For the next 0.7 mile, the trail descends a sandy gully then curves around to the left (north) and begins climbing. At 5.9 miles a FOLLOW WASH sign points up the wash as it again turns left. The only confusing point in this otherwise well-signed hike is encountered at mile 6.2 where a FOLLOW WASH sign points up the wash to the Mid Hills Campground and a signed trail leaves the gravelly wash to the right. Take the trail to the right. The FOLLOW WASH sign indicates a short loop return route for hikers starting at the Mid Hill Trailhead.

At 6.8 miles the trail passes a gate signed 1.2 MILES TO MID HILLS. The steadily climbing trail reaches a spring/seep. It then drops into a narrow gully and climbs steeply to the high point of 5,600 feet at 8 miles. The end-of-the-trail windmill can be seen from here. A gradual drop over the final 0.4 mile concludes this point-to-point traverse from Banshee Canyon to the Mid Hills in the middle of Mojave.

Miles and Directions

0.0 Start at the "Rings" trailhead at the Hole-in-the-Wall Picnic Area.

0.2 The steep descent to the canyon floor ends here.

0.3 Arrive at the mouth of Banshee Canyon.

1.0 At the signed trail junction with Wild Horse Canyon Trail, turn right toward the Mid Hills Campground.

2.2 Stay right at the trail junction.

2.4 Veer right at this trail junction.

2.5 The signed trail leaves the wash and turns left (north).

4.3 The trail crosses the Gold Valley Mine road; continue straight (north) and through a gate signed 3.8 MILES TO MID HILLS.

5.0 The trail crosses a fence signed MID HILLS 3.1 MILES.

5.9 At the FOLLOW WASH sign, turn left and proceed up the wash.

6.2 The signed trail leaves the wash to the right. A FOLLOW WASH sign points up the wash to the left to the Mid Hills Campground.

6.8 Arrive at a fence/gate signed 1.2 MILES TO MID HILLS.

8.0 Reach the high point at 5,600 feet.

8.4 Arrive at the signed endpoint at the Mid Hills trailhead next to the windmill.

9 Eagle Rocks

This is an easy stroll to a unique formation of monzogranite boulders.

See map on page 46.
Start: About 70 miles northwest of Needles.
Distance: 2 miles out and back (plus extra mileage for exploring the boulders and the valley between the piles).
Approximate hiking time: 1 to 2 hours.
Difficulty: Easy to the boulders; moderate for exploring boulder piles.
Trail surface: Dirt path with some rocks.
Seasons: November through May.
USGS topo maps: Columbia Mtn.-CA and Mid Hills-CA (1:24,000).
Trail contact: Hole-in-the-Wall Information Center (see appendix D).

Finding the trailhead: From Needles, drive 44 miles west on Interstate 40 to the Essex Road exit. Travel 10 miles northwest on Essex Road, then turn right on Black Canyon Road and continue for 10 more miles, passing Wild Horse Canyon Road. Continue north on Black Canyon Road another 5 miles and turn left onto the upper end of Wild Horse Canyon Road. Drive 2.8 miles to the first dirt road on your right after the Mid Hills Campground turnoff. Turn onto this unmarked dirt road, which occurs at the first sharp southward bend in Wild Horse Canyon. Drive 0.2 mile on the dirt road to a junction; park here if you don't have a four-wheel drive. Bear right and drive 0.1 mile to the wilderness boundary post at the end of the road on your right. Park at a wide spot on the road; the signed trail is your trail.

The Hike

The Eagle Rocks tower above the Mid Hills and are prominent beacons along the entire Kelso–Cima Road. These lumpy granite formations stand out in sharp contrast with the angular mountains in this central Mojave region. They beckon the curious hiker from afar but, oddly enough, disappear from sight as you approach the trailhead, obscured by the surrounding hills.

The hike heads downhill on a gentle, sandy trail, gradually mixing with a small wash, until the junction at 0.5 mile. It is not until 0.6 mile that the Eagle Rocks gradually appear. And what a surprise they are!

Much like the monzogranite of Joshua Tree National Park, these hulking boulders have rounded contours, immense size, and fantastic shapes. The powerful boulders tower 350 feet above the base of each pile. There are even Joshua trees on the hillsides near the boulder piles. This form of igneous rock is, upon closer inspection, quite chunky, resembling conglomerate with rectangular pieces of quartz imbedded in the surface. It provides great traction for adventuresome rock scramblers. Advanced rock-climbing skills are mandatory for the larger boulders, but novices can enjoy exploring the perimeter of the mounds.

The small valley between the two dominant boulder piles is an enchanting nook of wilderness to explore. A use trail leads 0.7 mile down the narrow valley,

Spires of Eagle Rocks' granite rise above the Mid Hills of Mojave National Preserve.

following a small wash. The canyon protects large piñon pines and live oaks from the strong winds that dwarf these species in more exposed locations nearby.

As you walk back along the trail to the parking area, you'll again be surprised at how quickly these granite obelisks disappear from view. Yet, as you travel around the preserve, you'll notice their prominence on the horizon.

Miles and Directions

0.0 Start at the trailhead, posted with a wilderness boundary marker at the dirt road.

0.5 At the junction with another trail, turn left uphill.

0.7 At the Y junction, either way is 0.1 mile to the granite fields; both are dead ends.

0.8 The trail dead-ends at the boulder fields. There's a faint use trail down the valley between the boulder piles.

2.0 Return to the trailhead.

10 Table Top Mountain Loop

This cross-country hike gets you on top of a distinctive, steep-sided butte in the heart of Mojave National Preserve. It can be done as either an out-and-back or loop hike. The ascent of the isolated flat-topped mesa provides a view of monzonite boulder formations and a 360-degree panorama of almost all of the preserve.

Start: About 70 miles northwest of Needles or 65 miles southeast of Baker.
Distance: 7-mile loop or out and back.
Approximate hiking time: 4 to 5 hours.
Difficulty: Strenuous.
Trail surface: Dirt trail and rocky wash, but most of route is cross-country.

Seasons: September through May.
USGS topo maps: Columbia Mountain-CA and Woods Mountains-CA (1:24,000).
Trail contact: Hole-in-the-Wall Information Center (see appendix D).

Finding the trailhead: From Baker, drive east on Interstate 15; take the Cima exit and head south on Cima Road for 28.5 miles to Cima Junction. Turn right (south) on Kelso-Cima Road and continue for 4.9 miles to Cedar Canyon Road; turn left (east) on Cedar Canyon Road and drive 6.4 miles to Black Canyon Road; turn right (south) on Black Canyon Road and drive 6.4 miles to the unsigned trailhead, which is on the east side immediately north of a cattle guard. Pull off on the east side of the road and park in a large turnaround camping area. The trail begins on an old dirt road on the northeast edge of the parking area.

From Needles drive 42 miles west on Interstate 40 and turn north onto Essex Road. After 10 miles turn north onto Black Canyon Road. Continue north 13.6 miles to the unsigned trailhead, which is on the right (east) side of the road just past a cattle guard. Park as described above.

Check on road conditions for Cedar Canyon and Black Canyon Roads, especially after rain or snow.

The Hike

There are a variety of approaches to Table Top Mountain, ranging from moderate to strenuous, but the final ascent to the summit is strenuous regardless of which route you choose. Table Top Mountain is bound by a private subdivision in Round Valley to the immediate north, posted against trespass. The park has purchased much of Gold Valley, but the 160-acre core, where there are homes, is privately owned. One of the advantages of this suggested route is that it takes place entirely on public land. The somewhat long 3.5-mile (one-way) approach traverses a variety of terrain with constantly changing views.

Begin by heading east up a draw on a clear trail that provides an easy start to an otherwise strenuous hike. Continue walking slightly downhill on the trail as it passes through a gate/fence at 0.3 mile. At 0.6 mile make a sharp left turn at a junction. The trail climbs up a wash next to an old broken waterline for another

Approaching the steep ascent of Table Top Mountain.

0.5 mile to a windmill/water tank used for watering cattle. An abandoned mine entrance and remnants of a mining road can be seen on the hillside to the left. A huge rock outcropping rises to the right, serving as a good landmark for the return trip along the base of the ridge. For point of reference, the windmill is the takeoff point for both the more difficult ridge-route loop and the base of the ridge out-and-back trip.

For the ridge route, proceed to the right along a fence, cross it, and climb northeast to the summit ridge behind and to the left of the previously mentioned large rock outcropping. To avoid trespassing on private land, keep to the right (south) side of the ridge. At 1.4 miles you'll likely end up close to a large rock cairn. From here climb straight up the ridge toward a prominent piñon pine on the horizon. At 1.7 miles and 5,700 feet, the ridge becomes very rocky but remains fairly level on a southeasterly line toward the flat-topped mountain. The ridge then drops to around 5,600 feet close to the wilderness boundary. For the next 0.4 mile, the going is difficult, requiring boulder scrambling, bushwhacking, and edging around sharp-spined yucca and other cacti. In general, skirt to the right of cliff faces and huge granite boulders.

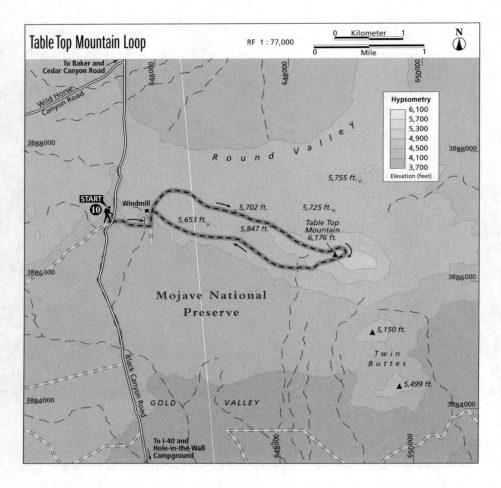

Table Top Mountain Loop

RF 1 : 77,000

0 Kilometer 1

0 Mile 1

N

Hypsometry
6,100
5,700
5,300
4,900
4,500
4,100
3,700
Elevation (feet)

To Baker and Cedar Canyon Road

Wild Horse Canyon Road

3888000

Round Valley

5,755 ft.×

3888000

START 10

Windmill

5,702 ft.

5,725 ft.×

5,653 ft.×

5,847 ft.

Table Top Mountain 6,176 ft.

3886000

3886000

Mojave National Preserve

▲ 5,150 ft.

Twin Buttes

▲ 5,499 ft.

Black Canyon Road

3884000

GOLD VALLEY

3884000

To I-40 and Hole-in-the-Wall Campground

At 2.8 miles the route becomes considerably easier with cow paths and side washes gradually climbing for 0.4 mile to the striking 5,810-foot western base of Table Top Mountain. The mountain is capped by sheer cliffs of dark lava atop a ring of white granite. The final 0.3-mile climb to the 6,176-foot summit is steep with loose rocks, but the route is direct and straightforward. Once you arrive at the base of the cliffs, the top is equally accessible by going either to the right or left and then up through a break in the cliffs. However, the route to the left (north) is somewhat faster.

On top, look for the peak register placed there in April 1983 by the Desert Peaks Chapter of the Sierra Club. The large plateau is well vegetated with sage, Mormon tea, rabbitbrush, and juniper. By all means walk along the rim for a chance to see raptors in the cliffs as well as ever-changing vistas. Table Top Mountain is strategically located between the jagged peaks of the Providence Mountains to the southwest and the rugged New York Mountains and Castle Peaks to the north.

Symmetrical Cima Dome fills the northwest horizon. Virtually all of the vast preserve can be seen from this central volcanic laccolith (plug).

For the return journey, ease your way down a break in the cliffs just west of the summit, proceeding cautiously on the steep, loose rock. After losing about 250 feet in 0.3 mile at the base of the steepest slope of the mountain, angle to the right (west) along a juniper-clad ridge. Continue dropping for another 0.4 mile to 5,600 feet in a wide upper wash encircled by piñon-juniper and boulders. At 0.9 mile the route crosses a bouldery draw: Drop to the left for another 0.4 mile to a flat bench at 5,300 feet.

For those going up on this route, look for a distinctive duck-head-shaped rock upslope and to your left.

At 1.6 miles cross a barbed-wire fence and angle northwesterly near the hillside on the right. At 2 miles the route passes just below the high pillar of rocks seen earlier from the windmill site. The windmill is visible straight ahead to the northwest. Continuing westward you'll soon intersect the trail. Go left and walk down to the trail junction, then turn right for the final 0.6 mile to the trailhead, thereby completing this exhilarating loop in Mojave's heartland.

Miles and Directions

0.0 From the trailhead, the trail heads east up a draw (5,180 feet).

0.3 Pass through a gate/fence.

0.6 Make a sharp left turn (north) at the junction.

1.1 The windmill/water tank marks the beginning of the cross-country route, with two options: Go north up the ridge of Table Top Mountain or hike along the base of the ridge.

Ridge Route:

1.4 Climb northeast to the summit ridge, keeping to the right side of the ridge to avoid private land.

1.7 Hike southeast along the ridge.

2.3 Skirt to the right below the cliff rocks.

3.2 Arrive at the base of Table Top Mountain.

3.5 Reach the summit (6,176 feet).

7.0 Return to the trailhead.

Base of Ridge Route:

1.9 Cross a barbed-wire fence.

2.2 Look upslope and left for a large duck-head-shaped granite rock. This is a good place to begin climbing toward Table Top Mountain.

3.2 Arrive at the southwest base of the mountain.

3.5 Reach the summit (6,176 feet).

7.0 Return to the trailhead.

11 Caruthers Canyon

Granite boulders and spires and an old mine site are tucked away up in Caruthers Canyon in the New York Mountains.

Start: About 65 miles northwest of Needles.
Distance: 3 miles out and back.
Approximate hiking time: 1 to 2 hours.
Difficulty: Moderate.
Trail surface: Rocky path.

Seasons: November through May.
USGS topo maps: Ivanpah-CA and Pinto Valley-CA (1:24,000).
Trail contact: Hole-in-the-Wall Information Center (see appendix D).

Finding the trailhead: From Needles, drive 45 miles west on Interstate 40 to the Essex Road exit. The Lanfair Road from Goffs is a shorter but far less traveled and maintained route. Travel another 10 miles northwest on Essex Road, then turn right on Black Canyon Road and continue another 10 miles to Wild Horse Canyon Road. Turn left for 1 mile and stop at the Hole-in-the-Wall Information Center to check on current road conditions. Then continue north on Black Canyon Road for another 10 miles to Cedar Canyon Road. Turn right and drive 15 miles to the Ivanpah/Lanfair intersection. Turn left (north) on Ivanpah Road and drive 5.7 miles to New York Mountain Road (signed). The turn is in a cattle feedlot for the OX Ranch and occurs right before a cattle guard. Drive 5.9 miles on New York Mountain Road and turn right onto an unmarked but well-traveled road into Caruthers Canyon. Continue north, disregarding a junction at 1.2 miles. At 1.8 miles locate a suitable place to leave your vehicle in the wide area before descending to the wash. The road from the wash at that point becomes progressively more impassable; the road instead becomes the hiking trail.

The Hike

The lush canyon bottom here is framed by spires of golden granite. A diverse plant community flourishes in Caruthers Canyon due to high elevation and plentiful water. There is also evidence of animal life, although, as in most desert habitats, it remains invisible during the day. Animal footprints around standing pools of water indicate their presence. If water is in Caruthers during your visit, please be considerate of the canyon's permanent residents and don't use the stream as a thoroughfare or play area. Desert water is too precious for such disrespect.

Your route is the old mine road to the Giant Ledge Mine. Like most roads of this kind, it exhibits remarkable engineering but is very rough. It is astonishing that it could be used by mine vehicles, especially ones loaded with ore. In the past decades it has deteriorated. It becomes increasingly rocky as you climb at 0.7 mile. Although the road is legally open since it is not in wilderness, nature is taking care of things and reclaiming it from the four-wheel-drive crowd with well-placed rock slides and fallen boulders. For a hiker, it also means slow going.

Numerous backcountry campsites dot the lower canyon. Some are tidy, but others show evidence of years of Bureau of Land Management's laissez-faire manage-

Granite mounds and spires rise within Caruthers Canyon in the New York Mountains.

ment, with scattered debris—broken glass, car parts, cans, bottles. The campsite on the spur at 0.2 mile is highly developed, with a cement table, barbecue, and fire ring. This is the work of an industrious camper!

The boulders of the canyon are certainly the most noteworthy focus of this trip. Fantastic balancing acts are everywhere. Twenty-ton boulders are frozen in a pirouette on 30-foot spires. Above the canyon on the eastern horizon is a hole-in-the-boulder that may grow to an arch eventually. The colors of the granite are as fascinating as the shapes. The central 300-foot granite mound has a golden tone, looking like a mound of petrified butterscotch. Your route curves around this formation, rising to the mine in the canyon above.

The mine site is a grotesque scar in this beautiful canyon. Massive tailing piles slump right into the creek bed below the mine. The hillside itself is pockmarked with gaping mouths of defunct mines. Be cautious near these, and do not go into them; often old mine shafts are unstable. The only equipment that remains is the chute used to deliver ore into the vehicles that carried it down the tricky mine road. The mine site provides a striking contrast with the natural beauty that surrounds it.

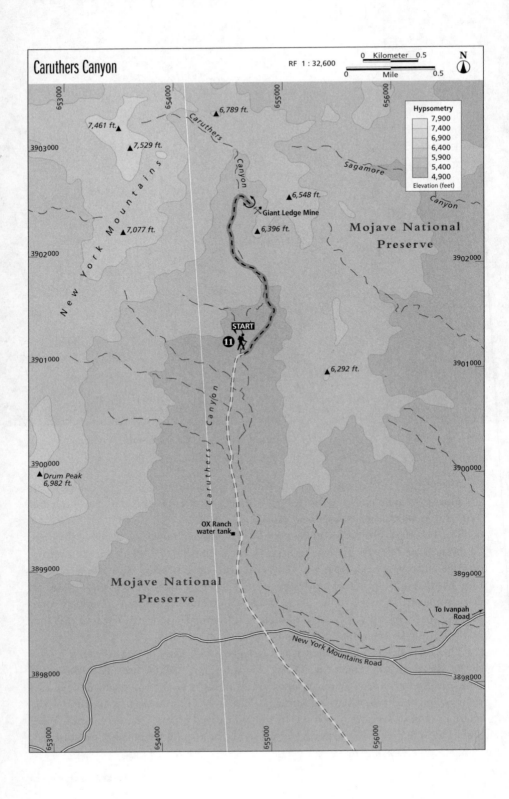

Caruthers Canyon

RF 1 : 32,600

0   Kilometer   0.5

0   Mile   0.5

N

Hypsometry

7,900
7,400
6,900
6,400
5,900
5,400
4,900

Elevation (feet)

▲ 6,789 ft.

7,461 ft. ▲

▲ 7,529 ft.

Caruthers

Canyon

Sagamore

Canyon

▲ 6,548 ft.

⚒ Giant Ledge Mine

▲ 7,077 ft.

▲ 6,396 ft.

Mojave National Preserve

New York Mountains

START

11 🚶

▲ 6,292 ft.

Caruthers Canyon

▲ Drum Peak
6,982 ft.

OX Ranch
water tank ■

To Ivanpah
Road

Mojave National Preserve

New York Mountains Road

After carefully looking around the mine site, return down the canyon to your vehicle at the mouth.

Miles and Directions

0.0 The trail begins at a wide wash.

0.2 Turn left at the fork. If you do explore to the right, you will find a well-appointed campsite.

0.8–0.9 Cross the wash, where there is often water in winter and spring.

1.5 Arrive at Giant Ledge Mine.

3.0 Return to the trailhead.

12 Keystone Canyon

This remote canyon in the rugged New York Mountains is bound by scenic granite towers and chaparral woodland that leads up to a historic mine.

Start: About 70 miles east of Baker and 77 miles northwest of Needles.

Distance: 3.8 miles out and back (with side-trip options ranging from a 0.5-mile out and back to an additional 4-mile out-and-back peak climb).

Approximate hiking time: 2 to 3 hours; additional 3 to 4 hours for peak.

Difficulty: Moderate for hike; strenuous for peak climb.

Trail surface: Rocky dirt two-track; off-trail to summit.

Seasons: October through May.

USGS topo map: Ivanpah-CA (1:24,000).

Trail contact: Kelso Depot Information Center (see appendix D).

Finding the trailhead: From Interstate 15, take the California Highway 164 exit and drive 3.6 miles east to Ivanpah Road. Turn right (south) and drive about 12 miles to Ivanpah, where the paved road changes to dirt. After another 6 miles turn right onto a rough unsigned road, for which four-wheel drive is recommended. Take another immediate right, passing the defunct Lecy Well. Stay to the right after 1 mile, then to the right on the main road. The unsigned trailhead/parking area is about 1.9 miles from Ivanpah Road, just before the road crosses the wash. This spot is a good campsite if you're planning to stay the night.

The Hike

Keystone is one of the premier canyons in the wild and rugged New York Mountains. Here you will find some of the most fascinating flora in the Mojave Desert—from chaparral brush fields to piñon–juniper and turbinella oak to lonely pockets of white fir clinging to windswept ridges. The New York Mountains host an amazing array of plants—some 300 species have been identified.

Granite spires tower above Keystone Canyon in the New York Mountains.

From the trailhead/parking area, the old two-track trail crosses the wash a few times before intersecting a mine road at 0.5 mile. Continue to the right up the main fork of the canyon, where you'll quickly pass Live Oak Canyon on your right. The view is striking, with granite spires punctuating the far horizon. On up the main canyon, an old rusty water pipe marks a trail on your left that leads 0.25 mile uphill to Keystone Spring. After hiking the old deteriorating two-track 1.9 miles, you'll have made the 1,000-foot climb from the trailhead to an old abandoned copper mine. Scattered boards and slag heaps tell the tale of shattered hopes from a mine that produced mostly dreams. Retrace your route to complete your exploration of this scenic gateway to New York Peak.

Miles and Directions

0.0 From the unsigned trailhead/parking area, the road crosses a wash.

0.5 At the junction with the mine road, continue to the right.

0.75 At the junction with Live Oak Canyon, continue to the left.

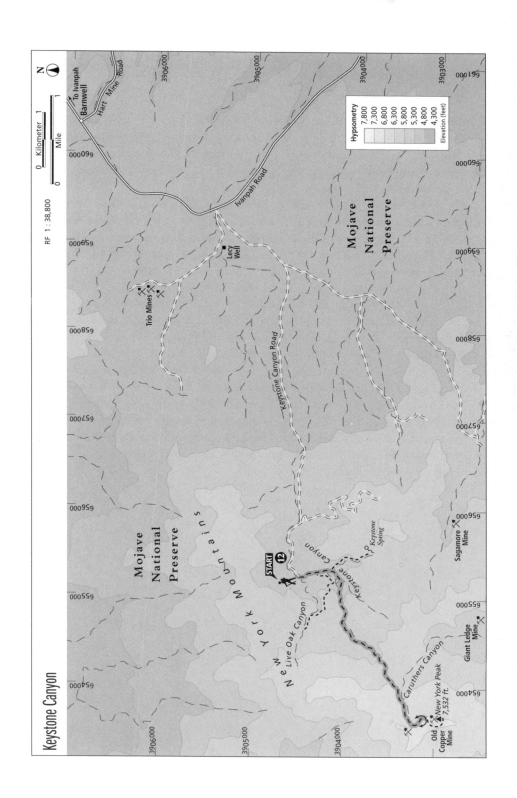

Keystone Canyon

RF 1 : 38,800

1.1 At the junction with the Keystone Spring trail, continue to the right.

1.9 The hike ends at the old copper mine. Retrace the trail to the trailhead.

3.8 Arrive back at the trailhead.

Options: Options off this main trail include a shorter excursion up *Keystone Canyon* to a grassy waterhole. This desert oasis is nestled in a steep, brushy north-facing draw up Live Oak Canyon from the main Keystone Canyon. Also, don't miss the easy 0.5-mile round-trip to Keystone Spring by way of an old mining trail that takes off 1.1 miles up the main-facing draw at 6,020-foot elevation.

Stone ruins—After the first mile on Keystone Canyon Road, take the first right-hand fork and continue another 0.5 mile; park next to a campsite. From here, take a short 0.5-mile round-trip hike up a small unnamed canyon just north of Keystone Canyon, bounded by hills dotted with piñon-juniper, cholla, and sage. You'll quickly come to picturesque stone walls, perhaps built by early cowboys.

A far more strenuous hike is an ascent of 7,532-foot-high *New York Peak,* the apex of the New York Mountains, climbing from the end of the Keystone Canyon hike at the old copper mine. This steep, challenging off-trail climb is only for experienced, well-conditioned hikers with route-finding ability. Be prepared for loose rocks and cliff faces that force an up-and-down route that is mostly parallel to the west ridge above the canyon. After gaining the north summit ridge to the peak, work your way south along the boulder-strewn divide to a rounded knob (7445 BM), just west of the rock columns that form the highest point in the range. Rock-climbing skills are needed to reach the actual top, especially during winter and early spring when snow in the cracks and fissures makes climbing both dangerous and difficult. From this lofty vantage point, you'll see the entire northeast quarter of the preserve—from radiating canyons to distant basins and ranges.

13 Fort Piute/Piute Gorge

This loop hike takes you to the only year-round stream in the East Mojave Desert. It retraces the route of early pioneers. Along the way, you visit the ruins of an army fort, view petroglyphs, and return via a dramatic gorge through the Piute Hills.

Start: About 74 miles northwest of Needles.
Distance: 7-mile loop.
Approximate hiking time: 3 to 4 hours.
Difficulty: Moderate to fort; strenuous return via gorge.
Trail surface: Dirt path, at times rocky; rocky wash.

Seasons: October through May.
USGS topo maps: Signal Hill-CA and Homer Mountain-CA (1:24,000).
Trail contact: Hole-in-the-Wall Information Center (see appendix D).

Finding the trailhead: From Needles, drive 37 miles west on Interstate 40 to the Fenner/Essex exit. (Call ahead for road conditions.) Continue 10 miles northeast to Goffs and turn left onto Lanfair Road. Drive another 16 miles north to the Cedar Canyon/Ivanpah/Lanfair Road junction. Make a right turn almost immediately onto a dirt road on your right with a small white PT&T sign. Head straight for a concrete building. Follow this road straight east for 3.9 miles, disregarding all other roads at intersections. At 3.9 miles turn right on an AT&T cable route and continue east to the Piute Hills. At 10.3 miles from the Ivanpah turnoff, turn left onto a marginal dirt road just before reaching a cattle guard. Proceed north for 0.5 mile and park in a wide turnaround marked with several rock cairns. The trail is the road that leaves this parking area and goes east to the ridge of the Piutes.

The Hike

Due to a human-caused fire in autumn 2004, Fort Piute, Piute Creek, and Piute Gorge were closed to visitors for one year to allow streamside vegetation to recover. The area has now reopened.

The Fort Piute/Piute Gorge hike is the perfect journey for the hiking party or the individual with diverse interests. It has petroglyphs for the archaeologist, an original Mojave Road segment for the emigrant historian, an old army fort for the military specialist, and a spectacular mile-long gorge for the geology enthusiast. The combination of all these aspects also makes it exciting for the generic adventurer.

The distance from the main road intersection at Cedar Canyon and the Ivanpah/Lanfair Road to the trailhead should not intimidate you. But these dirt roads were heavily rutted by winter 2005 rains. While it's virtually a straight shot 10.3 miles east to the Piute Hills from the intersection, a four-wheel-drive vehicle is necessary. Call for road conditions.

The counterclockwise loop, as described here, begins at the south trailhead. In doing the hike in this direction, you are walking down the Mojave Road (labeled

Old Government Road on the topo map) and not up, the way the emigrants did (unless you omit the gorge trip and return this way). While historically the eastward direction is incorrect, the Mojave Road would be an exercise in boredom after the magnificence of the Piute Gorge. This way the experiential height of the trip occurs on the trip out through the gorge—and the gorge is twice as impressive coming up from its lower eastern end.

The section of the hike (0.0 to 2.1 miles) on the Mojave Road is certain to create respect for the gutsy pioneers who used this thoroughfare. Built and guarded by the U.S. Army pursuant to our nineteenth-century policy to populate the West as quickly as possible, the Mojave Road followed an old Native American track. Be sure to pause at the saddle (0.2 mile from the trailhead), where the track is now closed to wheeled vehicles. Turn and look west. It is easy to relive the mixed feelings the emigrants must have had after struggling to reach this point, seeing the Mojave Desert stretching to the western horizon.

Hike on east down the Mojave Road. This segment rising from Fort Piute was known as one of the most arduous of the entire journey. As you will shortly discover, the volcanic rocks do not make a smooth road surface. Wagons without springs or shocks had a difficult time, as did the folks who had to walk along behind the Conestogas.

Where the road finally reaches the Piute stream are several petroglyph sites. Do not touch or deface them—leave them for others to enjoy.

When you reach the stream (2.1 miles), you'll revel in the lush vegetation, the watercress, and the sound of a gurgling brook. A considerate hiker does not use a riparian zone for a trail. Such use devastates vegetation and degrades the streambed. This resource is too precious for the desert residents to risk such destruction. Please use the trail high on the north bank instead. There's a more panoramic view from this high trail anyway.

Downstream 0.5 mile the ruins of Fort Piute are impressive for their remoteness. All that remain are the stone foundation of the blockhouse and a stone corral. Duty here must have been grim. The vista out over the Great Basin is endless. The emigrants traveling by this point had survived an incredible journey.

Heading back westward from the fort along the same high north-bank trail, the focus shifts to the mountain looming above. From this low point of the hike (2,700 feet), the Piute Hills look a lot more impressive than they do from the west, where they're a low line of hills—nothing in comparison to the Providence and New York ranges. Your trip through the gorge will change this perception forever. Traveling above the canyon and above Piute Spring gives you an eagle's view of the depth of the gorge 300 feet below. The descent into the gorge is neither arduous nor dangerous if you take the prescribed route (see mileage log). Be sure to stay up high until you nearly reach the mountainside and then travel down the side gorge, entering from the north just as the Piute wash disappears into the mountain.

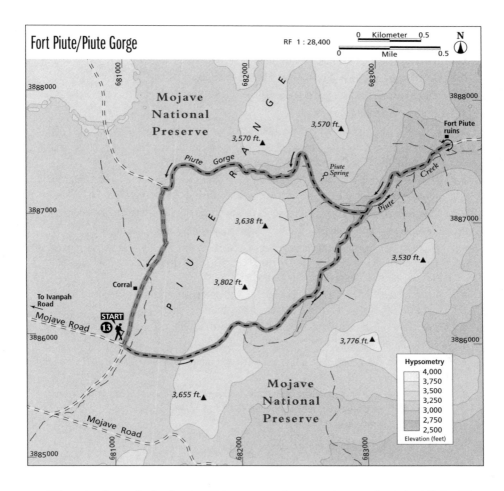

RF 1 : 28,400

0 Kilometer 0.5

0 Mile 0.5

N

3888000

681000

Mojave
National
Preserve

682000

E

G

N

A

R

3,570 ft.▲

3,570 ft.▲

683000

Fort Piute
ruins

3888000

Piute Gorge

R

Piute
Spring

Piute

Creek

3887000

681000

P

I

U

T

E

3,638 ft.▲

3,530 ft.▲

3887000

Corral ■

3,802 ft.▲

To Ivanpah
Road

Mojave Road

START
13 🚶

3886000

3,776 ft.▲

3886000

Hypsometry

3,655 ft.▲

Mojave Road

Mojave
National
Preserve

	4,000
	3,750
	3,500
	3,250
	3,000
	2,750
	2,500

Elevation (feet)

3885000

681000

682000

683000

The trip through the heart of the mountain range is a geologist's delight. The display of volcanic rock types, faulting and folding, and erosion is the most dynamic in the Mojave National Preserve. The peaks tower 600 feet above the sandy gorge floor. In places the gorge is no more than 10 feet wide. There are a few segments where stepping up a dry waterfall is necessary, but there is no boulder scrambling.

Like Alice in Wonderland, you emerge from the west entrance into a totally alien landscape. "Where am I?" is your first thought. The Mojave desert floor is 300 feet above the gorge exit, so the deeply eroded cliffs and mesas that greet you are unexpected. The well-cairned trail to the left, 0.1 mile from the gorge mouth, takes you back up to the familiar Mojave landscape, 1 mile north of where you started.

Whether your interests are Native Americans, emigrants, army recruits, or geology, this loop hike is sure to inspire you. It is definitely worth the long drive to the eastern edge of the preserve since it is unlike any other hike in the region.

Miles and Directions

0.0 Head east on the trail, which winds north along a fence.

0.2 Go through the gate and up the rocky trail to the ridge.

0.5 Reach the peak of the saddle (Piute Hill).

0.5–1.1 Hike down the Mojave Road.

1.1 Erosion has taken out the roadbed. Notice that the road drops into a wash to your right.

2.0 After the bend in the wash, at the reddish orange rocks, the road leads out of the wash to the left. This area has numerous petroglyphs. Be respectful.

2.1 At the streambed, cross and go upstream for 10 yards to cross in the willows and pick up the trail high on the north bank heading east. Do not use the streambed as a trail.

2.6 After reaching the fort ruins, turn around. Return on the north-bank trail to the intersection.

3.1 Continue west on the high bank trail. A large cutaway mountain is your beacon.

3.8 The trail seems to end at a crumbling precipice where you see the wash below turning and disappearing into the gorge. On the hill above you to the right are numerous cairns marking the trail. Climb and continue northwestward.

4.0 At the T intersection directly opposite the mouth of the gorge, take the well-cairned trail to the left, zigzagging down to a feeder canyon from the north.

4.2 Continue down the canyon to the main gorge/wash. Several dry falls require scrambling.

4.3–5.5 Hike up the gorge.

5.6 At the gorge exit, notice the cairn in the wash and others on your left marking the trail up from the canyon to the plateau above.

6.0 The trail comes over a crest to a parking area. Unless you have a driver to move your car for you, turn left and walk south on the dirt road that parallels the hills, by a cattle stockade, to the starting point.

7.0 Arrive back at the original parking area.

14 Castle Peaks

The volcanic turrets and spires of the Castle Peaks form a dramatic backdrop for unlimited exploration, adjacent to a rambling hiking corridor that penetrates deep into the remote northeast corner of the preserve.

Start: About 84 miles northwest of Needles.
Distance: 6.6 miles out and back (plus another 2 miles off-trail to the Castle Peak spires).
Approximate hiking time: 3 to 6 hours.
Difficulty: Moderate.

Trail surface: Sandy two-track trail and wash.
Seasons: October through May.
USGS topo map: Castle Peaks-CA (1:24,000).
Trail contact: Hole-in-the-Wall Information Center (see appendix D).

Finding the trailhead: From Needles, drive 37 miles west on Interstate 40 to the Fenner/Essex exit, then head northeast for 10 miles to Goffs. Turn left onto Lanfair/Ivanpah Road and drive 29 miles north to the junction with Hart Road (Barnwell historic site) and turn right (east). (Call for dirt road conditions.) If driving from the north from Interstate 15, take the California Highway 164 exit and drive 3.6 miles east to Ivanpah Road. Turn right (south) and drive about 12 miles to Ivanpah, where the paved road changes to dirt, then about 7 more miles to Barnwell. Turn left onto Hart Road. After driving 4.8 miles continue left (straight) for another 0.9 mile and turn left (north) onto the unsigned Castle Peak Road.

Drive another 2.8 miles to the end of the road near the signed wilderness boundary. Four-wheel drive is recommended for this rough road, and in particular the last mile requires a high-clearance vehicle. There is a large parking area and good campsite located about 100 yards before the end of the road. On the drive near the dam, watch for coveys of Gambel's quail.

The Hike

The aptly named Castle Peaks mark the northeast extension of that steep range of granite and limestone known as the New York Mountains. These jagged peaks are a cluster of dark red and brown spires streaked with white and are made up of volcanic andesite.

From the end-of-the-road wilderness boundary, follow an old grazing road that is gradually being reclaimed by the wilderness. The trail reaches a low divide at 1.3 miles, from which the views of the Castle Peaks continue to improve as you hike northward. This is classic high desert country with a varied mix of Joshua trees, Mojave yucca, and buckhorn cholla. The trail climbs a bit more to a saddle next to a distinctive granite dome on the left. The old roadbed ends abruptly just below the pass. Stay to the right and follow a wide sandy wash downhill. After another 0.5 mile the wash widens with a steeper gradient, bound by a surprisingly dense forest of Joshua trees. At this point several side washes have converged into the main wash. The lower wash is easy walking, bounded by occasional low walls of volcanic cliff rock with distant dark spires jutting up in every direction.

At 3.3 miles the trail ends at a stock tank and rustic old corrals—a picturesque

The Castle Peaks as seen from the trail.

remnant of the Old West. This is in one of the many recently retired grazing allotments in the preserve. The range already shows signs of recovery. For this varied 6.6-mile out and back, turn here and retrace your route to the trailhead. On the way back and close to the corrals, a two-track goes to the left. Keep to the right up the main wash. Stay to the right two more times as the wash splits en route to the saddle. At this point you'll pick up the old grazing road that leads back to the trailhead.

Miles and Directions

0.0 Start at the trailhead/wilderness boundary.

1.3 A two-track trail reaches the low divide.

1.6 At the high point the two-track trail ends. Follow the wash to the right.

2.7 Reach a confluence of side washes.

3.3 The corrals mark the end of the trail. Retrace your route to the trailhead.

6.6 Arrive back at the trailhead.

Options: *Castle Peaks Exploration*—After reaching the first rise at around mile 1.3, cross a fence and hike cross-country about 0.5 mile to the base of the highest spire.

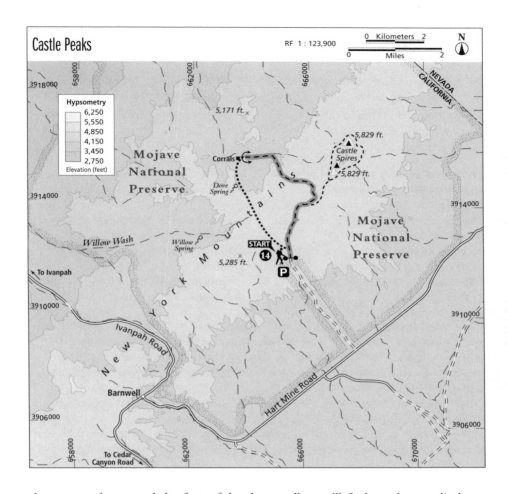

Castle Peaks

RF 1 : 123,900

Hypsometry
6,250
5,550
4,850
4,150
3,450
2,750
Elevation (feet)

5,171 ft.

5,829 ft.

Castle
Spires

5,829 ft.

Mojave
National
Preserve

Corrals

Dove
Spring

Mojave
National
Preserve

Willow Wash

Willow
Spring

START
14

5,285 ft.

P

To Ivanpah

Ivanpah Road

New York

Barnwell

Hart Mine Road

To Cedar
Canyon Road

NEVADA
CALIFORNIA

As you wander around the foot of the sheer walls, you'll find notches to climb up into for spectacular views framed by a wonderland of dark volcanic columns, pillars, spires, and turrets. Slopes are dotted with juniper, yucca, and scattered Joshua trees. Southward, the Lanfair Valley is ringed by distant mountain ranges stretching across the eastern flank of the preserve. This mile-high basin is home to a magnificent Joshua tree forest as well as a rich history of railroads, homesteads, and cattle ranches. You might spot golden eagles and other raptors as well as mule deer that find refuge in this rugged terrain. Plan on a pleasant 2- to 3-mile round-trip ramble to and around the base of the spires. With a roadside camp near the end of the road, you could spend a couple of interesting days exploring the Castle Peaks.

Dove Spring—From the corrals, an alternate but more strenuous return route would be to follow a side draw southwest for about 0.8 mile to Dove Spring. From there an experienced off-trail hiker can travel southeasterly up and down side ridges, winding around columns and pillars, eventually intersecting the lower end of the trail close to the trailhead.

15 Clark Mountain/North Canyon

At 7,929 feet Clark Mountain is the rooftop of the preserve. It is also an isolated enclave that is cut off from the main preserve by Interstate 15. Its elevation and isolation combine to make it the preserve's most distinctive landmark for many miles in every direction.

Start: About 43 miles northeast of Baker and 51 miles north of Kelso Depot.
Distance: 4.4 miles out and back (plus optional 5 to 6 miles out and back to the summit).
Approximate hiking time: 3 hours (optional 8 to 10 hours to and from peak).
Difficulty: Moderate in canyon; strenuous to peak.

Trail surface: Dirt and gravelly two-track for first 2 miles; steep, rocky, brushy bushwhack beyond.
Seasons: November through June for canyon hike; April through June for peak.
USGS topo map: Clark Mountain-CA (1:24,000).
Trail contact: Kelso Depot Information Center (see appendix D).

Finding the trailhead: From I-15, about 27 miles east of Baker, take the Cima Road/Excelsior Mine Road exit, turn left and drive north on the paved Excelsior Mine (Kingston) Road 7.7 miles to the graded Powerline Road. Turn right (east) and drive about 6 miles to a rougher road. Turn right (south) and drive about 2 miles to another dirt road that runs east-west along the north side of Clark Mountain. Continue left (east) for about 0.5 mile and park next to an old mining road at the lower end of the North Canyon valley. Four-wheel drive is recommended for the latter part of this route. The old road is blocked by the berm of the main road and by a wilderness boundary sign. There are no trailhead signs, so find a wide spot for parking. You can also access this spot from the east by driving west from the I-15 Yates Well exit, 5 miles south of Primm on the state line. But be warned. The steep, rocky, four-wheel-drive Colosseum Gorge Road is not for the faint of heart.

The Hike

From your jumping-off point near the wide valley mouth of Clark Mountain's north canyon, you'll have a panoramic view of the rugged north-face rim and amphitheater of the nearly 8,000-foot-high massif. This huge mountain, cut off from the rest of the preserve by I-15, has a long history of human use, including mining since the late nineteenth century. The most recent mining activity on the mountain slopes involved exploration for turquoise and copper during the 1990s. Today Clark Mountain is "rewilding," thanks to wilderness designation and sensitive nonmotorized use by the public.

Begin by hiking the two-track trail toward the walls of the upper North Canyon. The higher canyon is defined by a V-shaped notch below the formidable cliff rim of Clark Mountain. Despite its lofty elevation and north aspect, this is a

Clark Mountain is to the southwest when viewed from the east ridge.

waterless canyon, so carry plenty of water to drink. The two-track weaves up and through an alluvial fan dotted with piñon-juniper and agave. Ash-filled pits have been found on Clark Mountain where early natives roasted agave for food. Chemehuevi, Piute, and Mojave Indians lived here over the millennia, as evidenced by petroglyphs and rock shelters.

At 0.9 mile a side canyon enters from the right; continue left. At mile 1.6 the canyon narrows dramatically, with soaring volcanic cliffs pocketed with cave openings. Watch for bighorn sheep and mule deer. You might also see feral burros, a nonnative nuisance that might scold you with a loud bray just for being there. At 2 miles a massive wall forces the canyon sharply to the right. At this point the old roadbed ends and the narrow passageway becomes rough, rocky, and brushy. Look to the right for a faint game trail that climbs straight up to join a distinct path. The path drops to the canyon floor only to be blocked by a chokestone at mile 2.2. A series of steep chasms feed into the canyon here, making further up-canyon travel difficult to impossible. Retrace your route to complete this challenging exploration of the North Canyon.

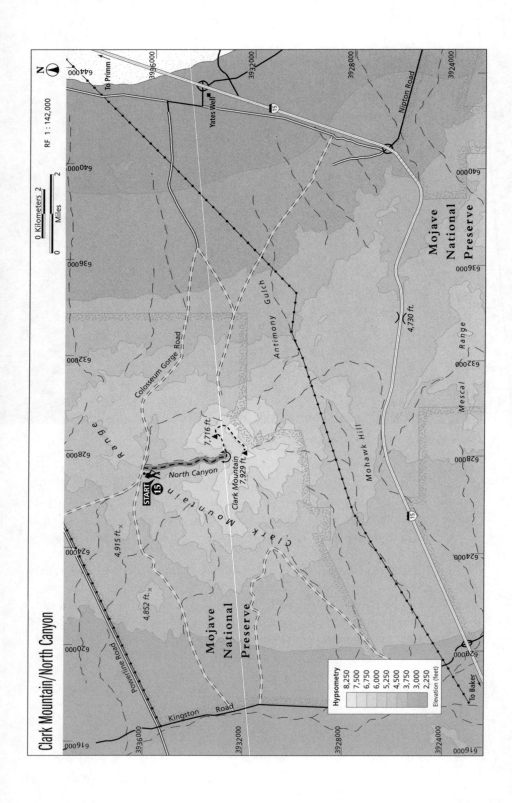

Clark Mountain/North Canyon

RF 1 : 142,000

Miles and Directions

0.0 Begin the hike from the wilderness boundary near the mouth of the canyon.

0.9 Where the canyon enters from the right, continue left.

1.6 The canyon narrows.

2.0 Reach the end of the old canyon roadbed.

2.2 Where the chokestone blocks the canyon, retrace your route to the trailhead.

4.4 Arrive back at the wilderness boundary.

Option: *Clark Mountain Northeast Ridge/Summit*—The peak can be climbed from this point by experienced, well-conditioned backcountry hikers. At the chokestone you've already gained 1,300 vertical feet from the trailhead, with a strenuous 1,700 feet remaining to the summit.

Begin the rock scramble by climbing straight up the left slope. You'll soon intersect a ridge that becomes more distinct as you gain elevation. The footing is loose, but handholds are solid, so long as they are carefully tested. Avoid cliffs by scrambling around slopes that are steep but usually well protected by vegetation. After about two hours of steady climbing, you'll reach a rocky point shown on the topo map as 2,352 meters (7,716 feet). From there you'll have an eagle's view of the entire north basin, rimmed by cliffs. On a clear day you'll see snowcapped Telescope Peak in Death Valley, along with numerous desert ranges far into Nevada's Great Basin.

From this rocky outcrop you can visualize a good cross-country route to the peak, which is still nearly 2 miles to the south. Drop to the nearby saddle and work up the steep side slope to the main northeast divide, and then onto the first false summit. Upon gaining the crest, the actual summit is an easy walk. Along the way you'll see stands of stately white fir gracing the higher ridges and north slopes.

The best way back down to the canyon bottom is the way you came up. Because of steep, unstable footing, the descent will take as long as the ascent. That's okay. Take your time to avoid injury. As you descend, look for feeder ridges and clear avenues to the right in order to bypass a particularly cliffy ridge that is higher and to the south. When at last you reach the canyon bottom, the gentle 2 miles back to the trailhead will seem like a cakewalk.

Afterword

As seasoned hikers accustomed to the high snowy mountains of the Northern Rockies we were excited when the idea of exploring some of the California Desert was presented to us. It would be hard to find two more disparate regions—the California Desert and the Northern Rockies—within the Lower 48. We viewed the opportunity to learn more about such a different ecosystem as a tremendous challenge. And we foresaw many interim challenges along the way, such as the challenge of truly getting to know this splendid country and its hidden treasures beyond the roads. There would be the challenges of climbing rugged peaks, of safely traversing vast expanses of open desert, of navigating across alluvial fans to secluded canyons, of learning enough about the interconnected web of desert geology, flora, and fauna to be able to interpret some of its wonders for others to appreciate. These beckoned to us from blank spots on the park map.

But we each face a far greater challenge—the challenge of wilderness stewardship, which must be shared by all who venture into the wilderness of the Mojave and California's other desert parks.

Wilderness stewardship can take many forms, from political advocacy to a zero-impact hiking and camping ethic to quietly setting the example of respect for wild country for others to follow. The political concessions that eventually brought about passage of the long awaited California Desert Protection Act have been made. Boundaries were gerrymandered, exclusions made, and nonconforming uses grandfathered. Still, the wilderness lines that have been drawn in Mojave National Preserve represent a tremendous step forward in the ongoing battle to save what little remains of our diminishing wilderness heritage.

But drawing lines is only the first step. Now, the great challenge is to take care of what we have. We can each demonstrate this care every time we set out on a hike. It comes down to respect for the untamed but fragile desert, for those wild creatures who have no place else to live, for other visitors, and for those yet unborn who will retrace our hikes into the next century and beyond.

We will be judged not by the mountains we climb but by what we pass onto others in an unimpaired condition. Happy hiking, and may your trails be clear with the wind and sun at your back.

Appendix A: Our Favorite Hikes

Mountains

Table Top Mountain Loop (10) Plateau with sweeping view of Mojave National Preserve

Clark Mountain/North Canyon (15) Twisting canyon, diverse forest, sweeping vistas

Open Desert

Hole-in-the-Wall to Mid Hills (8) Dramatic features and views

Castle Peak (14) Volcanic formations with sweeping views

Canyons

Fort Piute/Piute Gorge (13) Gorge hike through heart of mountain range

Waterfall and Stream

Caruthers Canyon (11) Seasonal brook with towering peaks

Prehistory and History

Fort Piute/Piute Gorge (13) Petroglyphs, Mojave Road, Fort Piute

Appendix B: Recommended Equipment

Use the following checklists as you assemble your gear for hiking the California desert.

Day Hike

- ❏ sturdy, well-broken-in, light- to medium-weight hiking boots
- ❏ broad-brimmed hat, which must be windproof
- ❏ long-sleeved shirt for sun protection
- ❏ long pants for protection against sun and brush
- ❏ water: two quarts to one gallon/day (depending on season), in sturdy screw-top plastic containers
- ❏ large-scale topo map and compass (adjusted for magnetic declination)
- ❏ whistle, mirror, and matches (for emergency signals)
- ❏ flashlight (in case your hike takes longer than you expect)
- ❏ sunblock and lip sunscreen
- ❏ insect repellent (in season)
- ❏ pocketknife
- ❏ small first-aid kit: tweezers, bandages, antiseptic, moleskin, snakebite extractor kit
- ❏ bee sting kit (over-the-counter antihistamine or epinephrine by prescription) as needed for the season
- ❏ windbreaker (or rain gear in season)
- ❏ lunch or snack, with baggie for your trash
- ❏ toilet paper, with a plastic zipper bag to pack it out
- ❏ your FalconGuide

Optional gear
- ❏ camera and film
- ❏ binoculars
- ❏ bird and plant guidebooks
- ❏ notebook and pen/pencil

Winter High-Country Trips

All of the above, plus:
- ❏ gaiters
- ❏ warm ski-type hat and gloves
- ❏ warm jacket

Backpacking Trips/Overnights

All of the above, plus:

- ❏ backpack (internal or external frame)
- ❏ more water (at least a gallon a day, plus extra for cooking—cache or carry)
- ❏ clothing for the season
- ❏ sleeping bag and pad
- ❏ tent with fly
- ❏ toiletries
- ❏ stove with fuel bottle and repair kit
- ❏ pot, bowl, cup, and eating utensils
- ❏ food (freeze-dried meals require extra water)
- ❏ water filter designed and approved for backcountry use (if the route passes a water source)
- ❏ nylon cord (50 to 100 feet for hanging food, drying clothes, etc.)
- ❏ additional plastic bags for carrying out trash

Appendix C: Other Information Sources and Maps

Natural History Association

Western National Parks Association (WNPA)
(covers Mojave National Preserve)
2701 Barstow Road
Barstow, CA 92311
(760) 733–4456
Web site: www.nps.gov/moja

This nonprofit membership organization is dedicated to the preservation and interpretation of the natural and human history western national parks, including Mojave Nation Preserve. Membership benefits include book discounts, educational programs, and periodic newsletters.

Other Handy Maps

Although the "At a Glance" chart lists only the detailed 7.5-minute topographic maps for each hike, the natural history association also sells additional maps that are indispensable for overall trip planning and for navigating around the park to and between hikes. These recommended maps are:

- The Bureau of Land Management (BLM) managed the East Mojave National Scenic Area before Congress awarded it national preserve status. The BLM 1:100,000 scale Desert Access Guides are valuable, not only for roads but also for determining land ownership. This is important because the preserve encompasses numerous private inholdings. Map guides covering the preserve include a California Desert District series from the BLM, 1999; the majority of the preserve is covered by the Amboy and Ivanpah maps. Books and maps can be purchased at Barstow, Kelso, and Hole-in-the-Wall.

- Mojave National Preserve, topographic backcountry and hiking map, 1:125,000 scale, published by National Geographic/Trails Illustrated

- AAA map of San Bernardino County published by the Automobile Club of Southern California

- Harrison map of Mojave

Appendix D: Park Management Agencies

Superintendent
Mojave National Preserve
2701 Barstow Road
Barstow, CA 92311
(760) 252–6100
Web site: www.nps.gov/moja

Kelso Depot Information Center
Mojave National Preserve
1924 Kelso-Cima Road
Kelso, CA 92309
(760) 733–4456
(Open year-round 9:00 A.M. to 4:00 P.M. Wednesday through Sunday.)

Hole-in-the-Wall Information Center
Black Canyon Road
Mojave National Preserve
P.O. Box 56
Essex, CA 92332
(760) 928–2572
(Open 9:00 A.M. to 4:00 P.M. Wednesday through Sunday from October through April; Friday through Sunday from May through September.)

For information about wilderness and other public lands adjacent to the preserve, contact:
Bureau of Land Management
Needles Field Office
101 West Spikes Road
Needles, CA 92363
(760) 326–7000

Providence Mountains State Recreation Area and Mitchell Caverns Natural Preserve (within the boundaries of Mojave National Preserve)
P.O. Box 1
Essex, CA 92332-0001
(760) 928–2586

Index

About the Authors

Polly and Bill Cunningham are married partners on the long trail of life. Polly, formerly a history teacher in St. Louis, Missouri, now makes her home with Bill in Choteau, Montana. She is pursuing multiple careers as a freelance writer and wilderness guide and working with the elderly. Polly has hiked and backpacked extensively throughout many parts of the country.

Bill is a lifelong "Wildernut," as a conservation activist, backpacking outfitter, and former wilderness field studies instructor. During the 1970s and 1980s he was a field rep for The Wilderness Society and Montana Wilderness Association. Bill has written several books, including *Wild Montana,* published by Falcon Press in 1995, plus numerous articles about wilderness areas based on his extensive personal exploration.

In addition to *Hiking Mojave national Preserve,* Polly and Bill have coauthored several other FalconGuide books, including *Wild Utah* (1998), *Hiking New Mexico's Gila Wilderness* (1999), *Hiking New Mexico's Aldo Leopold Wilderness* (2002) and *Hiking California's Desert Park* (2006).

Decades ago both Bill and Polly lived in California close to the desert—Bill in Bakersfield and Polly in San Diego. They enjoyed renewing their ties with California while exploring Mojave National Preserve for this book. Months of driving, camping, and hiking, with laptop and camera, have increased their enthusiasm for California's desert wilderness. They want others to have as much fun exploring this fabulously wide-open country as they did.

Authors Polly and Bill Cunningham